THE RETURN OF
DEPRESSION ECONOMICS
AND THE CRISIS OF 2008

More praise for

The Return of Depression Economics
and the Crisis of 2008

"Nobody who writes about economics does it better than Paul Krugman." —*Washington Post*

"Krugman's book is a call to action."
—Jonathan Rabinovitz, *San Jose Mercury News*

"Moving from concrete examples (e.g., the struggles of a Japanese baby-sitting coop) to stinging critiques of head-in-the-sand theorists, Krugman proves himself not only comprehensible but also well worth comprehending." —*Publishers Weekly*

"This is a brilliant book, but it scares me, for several reasons. . . . Krugman, a Nobel Prize–winning economist who specialises in recessions, takes us through the history of why they happen."
—William Leith, *The Guardian*

"To paraphrase biographer Richard Brookhiser's observation about Alexander Hamilton, Paul Krugman is a know-it-all who actually does seem to know it all." —J. Peder Zane, *The News & Observer*

"Reading Paul Krugman always makes me feel like a smarter person and a better citizen. As an economist with a common touch, he shares the ability with a couple of other specialized authors—Stephen Jay Gould and Carl Sagan—to make clear some very complicated concepts from a specialized subject area, and to make the reader enjoy the experience."

—Susan Gardner, *Daily Kos*

"Columnist and academic Paul Krugman is God of All Economic Thought in some Democratic literary and political circles. This midsize volume shows why. Krugman's facility both with arcane details and with vast unified explanations boils down complexity so much that the reader often wonders: Why didn't I see it that way myself? . . . Krugman's appeal, in this and the rest of his canon, lies in his gift at poking holes in economic cant and ideological explanations that don't fit real-world developments."

—Ross Kerber, *Boston Globe*

"Excellent. . . . Reading Krugman as he glances over the economic history of the past several decades is both enjoyable and thought-provoking." —Floyd Norris, *New York Times Book Review*

"A fascinating and extremely well written account of all the various booms and busts that our generation has witnessed. . . . This short book cannot help but improve the reader's understanding of the past 30 years of world economic history."

—Edwin T. Burton, *The Daily Progress*

"The man best able to explain the economic maelstrom."

—*San Francisco Chronicle*

"Almost certainly the world's most famous economist."

—Lionel Barber, *The Financial Times*

Paul Krugman

THE RETURN OF
DEPRESSION ECONOMICS
AND THE CRISIS OF 2008

W. W. Norton & Company   New York   London

For information about permission to reproduce selections from this book,
write to Permissions, W. W. Norton & Company, Inc.,
500 Fifth Avenue, New York, NY 10110

For information about special discounts for bulk purchases, please contact
W. W. Norton Special Sales at specialsales@wwnorton.com or 800-233-4830

Manufacturing by Courier Westford
Production managers: Andrew Marasia and Sue Carlson

Library of Congress Cataloging-in-Publication Data

Krugman, Paul R.
The return of depression economics and the crisis of 2008 / Paul Krugman.
p. cm.
ISBN 978-0-393-07101-6 (hardcover)
1. Recessions—History—21st century. 2. Business cycles—
History—21st century. 3. Financial crises—History—
21st century. 4. Depressions—1929. I. Title.
HB3716.K77 2009
330.9—dc22

2008048995

ISBN 978-0-393-33780-8 pbk.

W. W. Norton & Company, Inc.
500 Fifth Avenue, New York, N.Y. 10110
www.wwnorton.com

W. W. Norton & Company Ltd.
Castle House, 75/76 Wells Street, London W1T 3QT

1 2 3 4 5 6 7 8 9 0

Contents

THE RETURN OF
DEPRESSION ECONOMICS
AND THE CRISIS OF 2008

INTRODUCTION

M ost economists, to the extent that they think about the subject at all, regard the Great Depression of the 1930s as a gratuitous, unnecessary tragedy. If only Herbert Hoover hadn't tried to balance the budget in the face of an economic slump; if only the Federal Reserve hadn't defended the gold standard at the expense of the domestic economy; if only officials had rushed cash to threatened banks, and thus calmed the bank panic that developed in 1930–31; then the stock market crash of 1929 would have led only to a garden-variety recession, soon forgotten. And since economists and policymakers have learned their lesson—no modern treasury secretary would echo Andrew Mellon's famous advice to "liquidate labor, liquidate stocks, liquidate the farmers, liquidate real estate . . . purge the rottenness out of the system"—nothing like the Great Depression can ever happen again.

Or can it? In the late 1990s a group of Asian economies—economies that produced about a quarter of the world's output and were home to two-thirds of a billion people—experienced an economic slump that bore an eerie resemblance to the Great Depression. Like the Depression, the crisis struck out of a clear blue sky, with most pundits predicting a continuing boom even as the slump gathered momentum; as in the 1930s the conventional economic medicine proved ineffective, perhaps even counterproductive. The fact that something like this could happen in the modern world should have sent chills up the spine of anyone with a sense of history.

It certainly sent chills up my spine. The first edition of this book was written in response to the Asian crisis of the 1990s. Where some saw the crisis as a specifically Asian phenomenon, I saw it as a troubling omen for all of us, a warning that the problems of depression economics have not disappeared in the modern world. Sad to say, I was right to be worried: as this new edition goes to press, much of the world, very much including the United States, is grappling with a financial and economic crisis that bears even more resemblance to the Great Depression than the Asian troubles of the 1990s.

The kind of economic trouble that Asia experienced a decade ago, and that we're all experiencing now, is precisely the sort of thing we thought we had learned to prevent. In the bad old days big, advanced economies with stable governments—like Britain in the 1920s—might have had no answer to prolonged periods of stagnation and deflation; but between John Maynard Keynes and Milton Friedman, we thought we knew enough to keep that from happening again. Smaller countries—like Austria in 1931—may once have been at the mercy of financial tides, unable to control their economic destiny; but nowadays sophisticated bankers and government officials (not to mention the International Monetary

Fund) are supposed to quickly orchestrate rescue packages that contain such crises before they spread. Governments—like that of the United States in 1930–31—may once have stood by helplessly as national banking systems collapsed; but in the modern world, deposit insurance and the readiness of the Federal Reserve to rush cash to threatened institutions are supposed to prevent such scenes. No sensible person thought that the age of economic anxiety was past; but whatever problems we might have in the future, we were sure that they would bear little resemblance to those of the 1920s and 1930s.

But we should have realized a decade ago that our confidence was misplaced. Japan spent most of the 1990s in an economic trap that Keynes and his contemporaries found completely familiar. The smaller economies of Asia, by contrast, went from boom to calamity virtually overnight—and the story of their calamity reads as if it were taken straight out of a financial history of the 1930s.

At the time, I thought of it this way: it was as if bacteria that used to cause deadly plagues, but had long been considered conquered by modern medicine, had reemerged in a form resistant to all the standard antibiotics. Here's what I wrote in the introduction to the first edition: "So far only a limited number of people have actually fallen prey to the newly incurable strains; but even those of us who have so far been lucky would be foolish not to seek new cures, new prophylactic regimens, whatever it takes, lest we turn out to be the next victims."

Well, we were foolish. And now the plague is upon us.

Much of this new edition is devoted to the Asian crisis of the 1990s, which turns out to have been a sort of rehearsal for the global crisis now in progress. But I've added a lot of new material as well, in an effort to explain how the United States found itself looking like Japan a decade earlier, how Iceland found itself looking like Thailand, and how the original crisis countries of the 1990s have, to their horror, found themselves once again at the edge of the abyss.

About This Book

Let me admit at the outset that this book is, at bottom, an analytical tract. It is not so much about *what* happened as *why* it happened; the important things to understand, I believe, are how this catastrophe can have happened, how the victims can recover, and how we can prevent it from happening again. This means that the ultimate objective is, as they say in business schools, to develop the theory of the case—to figure out how to think about this stuff.

But I have tried to avoid making this a dry theoretical exposition. There are no equations, no inscrutable diagrams, and (I hope) no impenetrable jargon. As an economist in good standing, I am quite capable of writing things nobody can read. Indeed, unreadable writing—my own and others'—played a key role in helping me arrive at the views presented here. But what the world needs now is informed action; and to get that kind of action, ideas must be presented in a way that is accessible to concerned people at large, not just those with economics Ph.D.'s. Anyway, the equations and diagrams of formal economics are, more often than not, no more than a scaffolding used to help construct an intellectual edifice. Once that edifice has been built to a certain point, the scaffolding can be stripped away, leaving only plain English behind.

It also turns out that although the ultimate goal here is analytical, much of the writing involves narrative. Partly this is because the story line—the sequence in which events happened—is often an important clue to what theory of the case makes sense. (For example, any "fundamentalist" view of economic crisis—that is, a view that economies only get the punishment they deserve—must come to grips with the peculiar coincidence that so many seemingly disparate economies hit the wall in the space of a few months.) But I am also aware that the story line provides a necessary context for any attempts at explanation and that most people have not spent the last eighteen months obsessively following the unfolding drama. Not everyone recalls what Prime Minister Mahathir said in Kuala Lumpur in August 1997 and relates it to what Donald Tsang ended up doing in Hong Kong a year later; well, this book will refresh your memory.

A note about intellectual style: one temptation that often afflicts writers on economics, especially when the subject is so grave, is the tendency to become excessively dignified. Not that the events we are concerned with aren't important, in some cases matters of life and death. Too often, though, pundits imagine that because the subject is serious, it must be approached solemnly: that because these are big issues, they must be addressed with big words; no informality or levity allowed. As it turns out, however, to make sense of new and strange phenomena, one must be prepared to play with ideas. And I use the word "play" advisedly: dignified people, without a whimsical streak, almost never offer fresh insights, in economics or anywhere else. Suppose I tell you that "Japan is suffering from fundamental maladjustment, because its state-mediated growth model leads to structural rigidity." Well, guess what: I haven't said anything at all; at best I have conveyed a sense that the problems are very difficult, and there are no easy answers—a sense that may well be completely wrong. Suppose, on the other hand, that I illustrate Japan's problems with the entertaining tale of the ups and downs of a baby-sitting co-op (which will, in fact, make several appearances in this book). Maybe it sounds silly, maybe the levity will even offend your sensitivities, but the whimsicality has a purpose: it jolts the mind into a different channel, suggesting in this case that there may indeed be a surprisingly easy way out of at least part of Japan's problem. So don't expect a solemn, dignified book: the objectives here are as serious as can be, but the writing will be as silly as the subject demands.

And with that, let's begin our journey, starting with the world as it seemed to be, just a few years ago.

1

"THE CENTRAL PROBLEM
HAS BEEN SOLVED"

In 2003 Robert Lucas, a professor at the University of Chicago and winner of the 1995 Nobel Memorial Prize in Economics, gave the presidential address at the annual meetings of the American Economic Association. After explaining that macroeconomics began as a response to the Great Depression, he declared that it was time for the field to move on: the "central problem of depression-prevention," he declared, "has been solved, for all practical purposes."

Lucas didn't claim that the business cycle, the irregular alternation of recessions and expansions that has been with us for at least a century and a half, was over. But he did claim that the cycle had been tamed, to the point that the benefits of any further taming were trivial: smoothing out the wiggles in the economy's growth, he argued, would produce only trivial gains in public welfare. So it was time to switch focus to things like long-term economic growth.

Lucas wasn't alone in claiming that depression-prevention was a solved problem. A year later Ben Bernanke, a former Princeton professor who had gone to serve on the board of the Federal Reserve—and would soon be appointed as the Fed's chairman—gave a remarkably upbeat speech titled "The Great Moderation," in which he argued, much as Lucas had, that modern macroeconomic policy had solved the problem of the business cycle—or, more precisely, reduced the problem to the point that it was more of a nuisance than a front-rank issue.

Looking back from only a few years later, with much of the world in the throes of a financial and economic crisis all too reminiscent of the 1930s, these optimistic pronouncements sound almost incredibly smug. What was especially strange about this optimism was the fact that during the 1990s, economic problems reminiscent of the Great Depression *had*, in fact, popped up in a number of countries—including Japan, the world's second-largest economy.

But in the early years of this decade, depression-type problems had not yet hit the United States, while inflation—the scourge of the 1970s—seemed, finally, to be well under control. And the relatively soothing economic news was embedded in a political context that encouraged optimism: the world seemed more favorable to market economies than it had for almost ninety years.

Capitalism Triumphant

This is a book about economics; but economics inevitably takes place in a political context, and one cannot understand the world as it appeared a few years ago without considering the fundamental political fact of the 1990s: the collapse of socialism, not merely as a ruling ideology, but as an idea with the power to move men's minds.

That collapse began, rather oddly, in China. It is still mind-boggling to realize that Deng Xiaoping launched his nation on what turned out to be the road to capitalism in 1978, only three years after the Communist victory in Vietnam, only two years after the internal defeat of radical Maoists who wanted to resume the Cultural Revolution. Probably Deng did not fully realize how far that road would lead; certainly it took the rest of the world a long time to grasp that a billion people had quietly abandoned Marxism. In fact, as late as the early 1990s China's transformation had failed fully to register with the chattering classes; in the best-sellers of the time, the world economy was an arena for "head to head" struggle between Europe, America, and Japan—China was thought of, if at all, as a subsidiary player, perhaps part of an emerging yen bloc.

Nonetheless, everyone realized that something had changed, and that "something" was the collapse of the Soviet Union.

Nobody really understands what happened to the Soviet regime. With the benefit of hindsight we now think of the whole structure as a sort of ramshackle affair, doomed to eventual failure. Yet this was a regime that had maintained its grip through civil war and famine, that had been able against terrible odds to defeat the Nazis, that was able to mobilize the scientific and industrial resources to contest America's nuclear superiority. How it could have ended so suddenly, not with a bang but with a whimper, should be regarded as one of the great puzzles of political economy. Maybe it was simply a matter of time—it seems that revolutionary fervor, above all the willingness to murder your opponents in the name of the greater good, cannot last more than a couple of generations. Or maybe the regime was gradually undermined by the stubborn refusal of capitalism to display the proper degree of decadence: I have a private theory, based on no evidence whatsoever, that the rise of Asia's capitalist economies subtly but deeply demoralized the Soviet regime, by making its claim to have history on its side ever less plausible. A debilitating, unwinnable war in Afghanistan certainly helped the process along, as did the evident inability of Soviet industry to match Ronald Reagan's arms buildup. Whatever the reasons, in 1989 the Soviet empire in Eastern Europe suddenly unraveled, and in 1991 so did the Soviet Union itself.

The effects of that unraveling were felt around the world, in ways obvious and subtle. And all of the effects were favorable to the political and ideological dominance of capitalism.

First of all, of course, several hundred million people who had lived under Marxist regimes suddenly became citizens of states prepared to give markets a chance. Somewhat surprisingly, however, this has in some ways turned out to be the least important consequence of the Soviet collapse. Contrary to what most people expected, the "transition economies" of Eastern Europe did not quickly become a major force in the world market, or a favored destination for foreign investment. On the contrary, for the most part they had a very hard time making the transition: East Germany, for example, has become Germany's equivalent of Italy's Mezzogiorno, a permanently depressed region that is a continual source of social and fiscal concern. Only now, almost two decades after the fall of Communism, are a few countries—Poland, Estonia, the Czech Republic—starting to look like success stories. And Russia itself has become a surprisingly powerful source of financial and political instability for the rest of the world. But let's reserve that story for Chapter 6.

Another direct effect of the collapse of the Soviet regime was that other governments that had relied on its largesse were now on their own. Since some of these states had been idealized and idolized by opponents of capitalism, their sudden poverty—and the corresponding revelation of their previous dependency—helped to undermine the legitimacy of all such movements. When Cuba seemed a heroic nation, standing alone with clenched fist confronting the United States, it was an attractive symbol for revolutionaries across Latin America—far more attractive, of course, than the gray bureaucrats of Moscow. The shabbiness of post-Soviet Cuba is not only disillusioning in itself; it makes painfully clear that the heroic stance of the past was possible only because of huge subsidies from those very bureaucrats. Similarly, until the 1990s North Korea's government, for all its ghastliness, held a certain mystique for radicals, particularly among South Korean students. With its population literally starving because it no longer receives Soviet aid, the thrill is gone.

Yet another more or less direct effect of Soviet collapse was the disappearance of the many radical movements that, whatever their claims to represent a purer revolutionary spirit, were in fact able to operate only because Moscow provided the weapons, the training camps, and the money. Europeans like to point out that the radical terrorists of the seventies and eighties—Baader-Meinhof in Germany, the Red Army Brigades in Italy—all claimed to be true Marxists, unconnected with the corrupt old Communists in Russia. Yet we now know that they were deeply dependent on Soviet-bloc aid, and as soon as that aid vanished, so did the movements.

Most of all, the humiliating failure of the Soviet Union destroyed the socialist dream. For a century and a half the idea of socialism—from each according to his abilities, to each according to his needs—served as an intellectual focal point for those who disliked the hand the market dealt them. Nationalist leaders invoked socialist ideals as they blocked foreign investment or repudiated foreign debts; labor unions used the rhetoric of socialism as they demanded higher wages; even businessmen appealed to vaguely socialist principles when demanding tariffs or subsidies. And those governments that nonetheless embraced more or less free markets did so cautiously, a bit shamefacedly, because they always feared that too total a commitment to letting markets have their way would be seen as a brutal, inhumane, anti-*social* policy.

But who can now use the words of socialism with a straight face? As a member of the baby boomer generation, I can remember when the idea of revolution, of brave men pushing history forward, had a certain glamour. Now it is a sick joke: after all the purges and gulags, Russia was as backward and corrupt as ever; after all the Great Leaps and Cultural Revolutions, China decided that making money is the highest good. There are still radical leftists out there, who stubbornly claim that true socialism has not yet been tried; and there are still moderate leftists, who claim with more justification that one can reject Marxist-Leninism without necessarily becoming a disciple of Milton Friedman. But the truth is that the heart has gone out of the opposition to capitalism.

For the first time since 1917, then, we live in a world in which property rights and free markets are viewed as fundamental principles, not grudging expedients; where the unpleasant aspects of a market system—inequality, unemployment, injustice—are accepted as facts of life. As in the Victorian era, capitalism is secure not only because of its successes—which, as we will see in a moment, have been very real—but because nobody has a plausible alternative.

This situation will not last forever. Surely there will be other ideologies, other dreams; and they will emerge sooner rather than later if the current economic crisis persists and deepens. But for now capitalism rules the world unchallenged.

The Taming of the Business Cycle

The great enemies of capitalist stability have always been war and depression. War, needless to say, is still with us. But the wars that almost brought capitalism to an end in the middle years of the twentieth century were giant conflicts among great powers—and it's hard to see how that kind of war could erupt in the foreseeable future.

What about depression? The Great Depression came close to destroying both capitalism and democracy, and led more or less directly to war. It was followed, however, by a generation of sustained economic growth in the industrial world, during which recessions were short and mild, recoveries strong and sustained. By the late 1960s the United States had gone so long without a recession that economists were holding conferences with titles like "Is the Business Cycle Obsolete?"

The question was premature: the 1970s was the decade of "stagflation," economic slump and inflation combined. The two energy crises of 1973 and 1979 were followed by the worst recessions since the 1930s. But by the 1990s the question was being asked again; and as we just saw, both Robert Lucas and Ben Bernanke went on record a few years ago with the claim that while the economy would continue to suffer from occasional setbacks, the days of really severe recessions, let alone worldwide depressions, were behind us.

How would you make up your mind about such a claim, other than by noticing that the economy has not had a major recession lately? To answer that question we need to make a digression into theory and ask ourselves what the business cycle is all about. In particular, why do market economies experience recessions?

Whatever you do, don't say that the answer is obvious—that recessions occur because of X, where X is the prejudice of your choice. The truth is that if you think about it—especially if you understand and generally believe in the idea that markets usually manage to match supply and demand—a recession is a very peculiar thing indeed. For during an economic slump, especially a severe one, supply seems to be everywhere and demand nowhere. There are willing workers but not enough jobs, perfectly good factories but not enough orders, open shops but not enough customers. It's easy enough to see how there can be a shortfall of demand for *some* goods: if manufacturers produce a lot of Barbie dolls, but it turns out that consumers want Bratz instead, some of those Barbies may go unsold. But how can there be too little demand for goods in general? Don't people have to spend their money on *something*?

Part of the problem people have in talking sensibly about recessions is that it is hard to picture what is going on during a slump, to reduce it to a human scale. But I have a favorite story that I like to use, both to explain what recessions are all about and as an "intuition pump" for my own thought. (Readers of my earlier books have heard this one before.) It is a true story, although in Chapter 3 I will use an imaginary elaboration to try to make sense of Japan's malaise.

The story is told in an article by Joan and Richard Sweeney, published in 1978 under the title "Monetary Theory and the Great Capitol Hill Baby-sitting Co-op Crisis." Don't recoil at the title: this is serious.

During the 1970s the Sweeneys were members of, surprise, a baby-sitting cooperative: an association of young couples, in this case mainly people with congressional jobs, who were willing to baby-sit each other's children. This particular co-op was unusually large, about 150 couples, which meant not only that there were plenty of potential baby-sitters but also that managing the organization—especially making sure that each couple did its fair share—was not a trivial matter.

Like many such institutions (and other barter schemes), the Capitol Hill co-op dealt with the problem by issuing scrip: coupons entitling the bearer to one hour of baby-sitting. When babies were sat, the baby-sitters would receive the appropriate number of coupons from the baby-sittees. This system was, by construction, shirkproof: it automatically ensured that over time each couple would provide exactly as many hours of baby-sitting as it received.

But it was not quite that simple. It turns out that such a system requires a fair amount of scrip in circulation. Couples with several free evenings in a row, and no immediate plans to go out, would try to accumulate reserves for the future; this accumulation would be matched by the running down of other couples' reserves, but over time each couple would on the average probably want to hold enough coupons to go out several times between bouts of baby-sitting. The issuance of coupons in the Capitol Hill co-op was a complicated affair: couples received coupons on joining, were supposed to repay them on leaving, but also paid dues in baby-sitting coupons that were used to pay officers, and so on. The details aren't important; the point is that there came a time when relatively few coupons were in circulation—too few, in fact, to meet the co-op's needs.

The result was peculiar. Couples who felt their reserves of coupons to be insufficient were anxious to baby-sit and reluctant to go out. But one couple's decision to go out was another's opportunity to baby-sit; so opportunities to baby-sit became hard to find, making couples even more reluctant to use their reserves except on special occasions, which made baby-sitting opportunities even scarcer . . .

In short, the co-op went into a recession.

Okay, time out. How do you react to being told this story?

If you are baffled—wasn't this supposed to be a book about the world economic crisis, not about child care?—you have missed the point. The only way to make sense of any complex system, be it global weather or the global economy, is to work with models— simplified representations of that system which you hope help you understand how it works. Sometimes models consist of systems of equations, sometimes of computer programs (like the simulations that give you your daily weather forecast); but sometimes they are like the model airplanes that designers test in wind tunnels, small-scale versions of the real thing that are more accessible to observation and experiment. The Capitol Hill Baby-sitting Co-op was a miniature economy; it was indeed just about the smallest economy capable of having a recession. But what it experienced *was* a real recession, just as the lift generated by a model airplane's wings is real lift; and just as the behavior of that model can give designers valuable insights into how a jumbo jet will perform, the ups and downs of the co-op can give us crucial insights into why full-scale economies succeed or fail.

If you are not so much puzzled as offended—we're supposed to be discussing important issues here, and instead you are being told cute little parables about Washington yuppies—shame on you. Remember what I said in the introduction: whimsicality, a willingness to play with ideas, is not merely entertaining but essential in times like these. Never trust an aircraft designer who refuses to play with model airplanes, and never trust an economic pundit who refuses to play with model economies.

As it happens, the tale of the baby-sitting co-op will turn out to be a powerful tool for understanding the not-at-all-whimsical problems of real-world economies. The theoretical models economists use, mainly mathematical constructs, often sound far more complicated than this; but usually their lessons can be translated into simple parables like that of the Capitol Hill co-op (and if they can't, often this is a sign that something is wrong with the model). I will end up returning to the baby-sitting story several times in this book, in a variety of contexts. For now, however, let's consider two crucial implications of the story: one about how recessions can happen, the other about how to deal with them.

First, why did the baby-sitting co-op get into a recession? It was *not* because the members of the co-op were doing a bad job of baby-sitting: maybe they were, maybe they weren't, but anyway that is a separate issue. It wasn't because the co-op suffered from "Capitol Hill values," or engaged in "crony baby-sittingism," or had failed to adjust to changing baby-sitting technology as well as its competitors. The problem was not with the co-op's ability to produce, but simply a lack of "effective demand": too little spending on real goods (baby-sitting time) because people were trying to accumulate cash (baby-sitting coupons) instead. The lesson for the real world is that your vulnerability to the business cycle may have little or nothing to do with your more fundamental economic strengths and weaknesses: bad things can happen to good economies.

Second, in that case, what was the solution? The Sweeneys report that in the case of the Capitol Hill co-op it was quite difficult to convince the governing board, which consisted mainly of lawyers, that the problem was essentially technical, with an easy fix. The co-op's officers at first treated it as what an economist would call a "structural" problem, requiring direct action: a rule was passed *requiring* each couple to go out at least twice a month. Eventually, however, the economists prevailed, and the supply of coupons was increased. The results were magical: with larger reserves of coupons couples became more willing to go out, making opportunities to baby-sit more plentiful, making couples even more willing to go out, and so on. The co-op's GBP—gross baby-sitting product, measured in units of babies sat—soared. Again, this was not because the couples had become better baby-sitters, or that the co-op had gone through any sort of fundamental reform process; it was simply because the monetary screwup had been rectified. Recessions, in other words, can be fought simply by printing money—and can sometimes (usually) be cured with surprising ease.

And with that let us return to the business cycle in the full-scale world.

The economy of even a small nation is, of course, far more complex than that of a baby-sitting co-op. Among other things, people in the larger world spend money not only for their current pleasure but also to invest for the future (imagine hiring co-op members not to watch your babies but to build a new playpen). And in the big world there is also a capital market in which those with spare cash can lend it at interest to those who need it now. But the fundamentals are the same: a recession is normally a matter of the public as a whole trying to accumulate cash (or, what is the same thing, trying to save more than it invests) and can normally be cured simply by issuing more coupons.

The coupon issuers of the modern world are known as central banks: the Federal Reserve, the European Central Bank, the Bank of Japan, and so on. And it is their job to keep the economy on an even keel by adding or subtracting cash as needed.

But if it's that easy, why do we ever experience economic slumps? Why don't the central banks always print enough money to keep us at full employment?

Before World War II, policymakers, quite simply, had no idea what they were supposed to be doing. Nowadays practically the whole spectrum of economists, from Milton Friedman leftward, agrees that the Great Depression was brought on by a collapse of effective demand and that the Federal Reserve should have fought the slump with large injections of money. But at the time this was by no means the conventional wisdom. Indeed, many prominent economists subscribed to a sort of moralistic fatalism, which viewed the Depression as an inevitable consequence of the economy's earlier excesses, and indeed as a healthy process: recovery, declared Joseph Schumpeter, "is sound only if it [comes] of itself. For any revival which is merely due to artificial stimulus leaves part of the work of depressions undone and adds, to an undigested remnant of maladjustment, new maladjustment of its own which has to be liquidated in turn, thus threatening business with another [worse] crisis ahead."

Such fatalism vanished after the war, and for a generation most countries did try actively to control the business cycle, with considerable success; recessions were mild, and jobs were usually plentiful. By the late 1960s many started to believe that the business cycle was no longer a major problem; even Richard Nixon promised to "fine-tune" the economy.

This was hubris, and the tragic flaw of full-employment policies became apparent in the 1970s. If the central bank is overoptimistic about how many jobs can be created, if it puts too much money into circulation, the result is inflation. And once that inflation has become deeply embedded in the public's expectations, it can be wrung out of the system only through a period of high unemployment. Add in some external shock that suddenly increases prices—such as a doubling of the price of oil—and you have a recipe for nasty, if not Depression-sized, economic slumps.

But by the middle of the 1980s inflation had fallen back to tolerable levels, oil was in abundant supply, and central bankers finally seemed to be getting the hang of economic management. Indeed,

the shocks the economy experienced seemed, if anything, to rein-
force the sense that we had finally figured this thing out. In 1987,
for example, the U.S. stock market crashed—with a one-day fall
that was as bad as the first day's fall of the 1929 crash. But the
Federal Reserve pumped cash into the system, the real economy
didn't even slow down, and the Dow soon recovered. At the end of
the 1980s central bankers, worried about a small rise in inflation,
missed the signs of a developing recession and got behind the curve
in fighting it; but while that recession cost George H. W. Bush his
job, eventually it responded to the usual medicine, and the United
States entered into another period of sustained expansion. By the
late 1990s it seemed safe to say that the business cycle, if it had not
been eliminated, had at least been decisively tamed.

Much of the credit for that taming went to the money managers:
never in history has a central banker enjoyed the mystique of Alan
Greenspan. But there was also a sense that the underlying structure of the economy had changed in ways that made continuing
prosperity more likely.

Technology as Savior

In a strict technological sense you could say that the modern information age began when Intel introduced the microprocessor—the
guts of a computer on a single chip—back in 1971. By the early
1980s products that put this technology to highly visible use—fax
machines, video games, and personal computers—were becoming
widespread. But at the time it didn't feel like a revolution. Most
people assumed that the information industries would continue to
be dominated by big, bureaucratic companies like IBM—or that
all of the new technologies would eventually go the way of the fax
machine, the VCR, and the video game: invented by innovative

Americans but converted into a paying product only by faceless Japanese manufacturers.

By the nineties, however, it was clear that the information industries would dramatically change the look and feel of our economy.

It is still possible to be skeptical about how large the ultimate economic benefits of information technology will be. What cannot be denied is that the new technologies have had a more *visible* impact on how we work than anything in the previous twenty or thirty years. The typical modern American worker, after all, now sits in an office; and from 1900 until the 1980s the basic appearance of and working of a business office—typewriters and file cabinets, memos and meetings—was pretty much static. (Yes, the Xerox machine did do away with carbon paper.) Then, over a fairly short time, the whole thing changed: networked PCs on every desk, e-mail and the Internet, videoconferencing and telecommuting. This was qualitative, unmistakable change, which created a sense of major progress in a way that mere quantitative improvements could not. And that sense of progress helped bring with it a new sense of optimism about capitalism.

Moreover, the new industries brought back what we might call the romance of capitalism: the idea of the heroic entrepreneur who builds a better mousetrap, and in so doing becomes deservedly wealthy. Ever since the days of Henry Ford, that heroic figure had come to seem ever more mythical, as the economy became increasingly dominated by giant corporations, run not by romantic innovators but by bureaucrats who might just as well have been government officials. In 1968 John Kenneth Galbraith wrote, "With the rise of the modern corporation, the emergence of the organization required by modern technology and planning and the divorce of the owner of capital from control of the enterprise, the entrepreneur no longer exists as an individual person in the mature industrial enterprise." And who could be enthusiastic about capitalism that seemed more or less like socialism without the justice?

The information industries, however, shook up the industrial order. As in the nineteenth century, the economic story became one of remarkable individuals: of men (and, at least occasionally, women) who had a better idea, developed it in their garage or on their kitchen table, and struck it rich. Business magazines actually became interesting to read; and business success came to seem admirable, in a way that it hadn't for more than a century.

And this provided fertile ground for free-market ideas. Forty years ago, defenders of the free market, of the virtues of untrammeled entrepreneurship, had an image problem: when they said "private enterprise," most people thought of General Motors; when they said "businessman," most people thought of the man in the gray flannel suit. In the 1990s the old idea that wealth is the product of virtue, or at least of creativity, made a comeback.

But what really fed economic optimism was the remarkable spread of prosperity—not merely to the advanced nations (where, indeed, the benefits were not as widely spread as one might have wished) but to many countries that not long ago had been written off as economically hopeless.

The Fruits of Globalization

The term "Third World" was originally intended as a badge of pride: Jawaharlal Nehru coined it to refer to those countries that maintained their independence, allying themselves neither with the West nor with the Soviet Union. But soon enough the political intention was overwhelmed by the economic reality: "Third World" came to mean backward, poor, less developed. And the term came to carry a connotation not of righteous demand but of hopelessness.

What changed all of that was globalization: the transfer of technology and capital from high-wage to low-wage countries, and the resulting growth of labor-intensive Third World exports.

It is a bit hard to remember what the world looked like before globalization; so let's try to turn the clock back for a moment, to the Third World as it was a generation ago (and still is, in many countries). In those days, although the rapid economic growth of a handful of small East Asian nations had started to attract attention, developing countries like the Philippines, or Indonesia, or Bangladesh were still mainly what they had always been: exporters of raw materials, importers of manufactures. Small, inefficient manufacturing sectors served their domestic markets, sheltered behind import quotas, but these sectors generated few jobs. Meanwhile, population pressure pushed desperate peasants into cultivating ever more marginal land, or into seeking a livelihood in any way possible, such as homesteading on the mountains of garbage found near many Third World cities.

Given this lack of other opportunities, you could hire workers in Djakarta or Manila for a pittance. But in the mid-1970s cheap labor was not enough to allow a developing country to compete in world markets for manufactured goods. The entrenched advantages of advanced nations—their infrastructure and technical know-how, the vastly larger size of their markets and their proximity to suppliers of key components, their political stability and the subtle but crucial social adaptations that are necessary to operate an efficient economy—seemed to outweigh even a ten- or twentyfold disparity in wage rates. Even radicals seemed to despair of reversing those entrenched advantages: in the 1970s demands for a New International Economic Order were centered on attempts to increase the price of raw materials, rather than to bring Third World countries into the modern industrial world.

And then something changed. Some combination of factors that we still don't fully understand—lower tariff barriers, improved tele-communications, the advent of cheap air transport—reduced the disadvantages of producing in developing countries. Other things being the same, it is still better to produce in the First World—stories of firms that moved production to Mexico or East Asia, then decided to move back after experiencing the disadvantages of the Third World environment at first hand are actually quite common—but there were now a substantial number of industries in which low wages gave developing countries enough of a com-petitive advantage to break into world markets. And so countries that previously made a living selling jute or coffee started produc-ing shirts and sneakers instead.

Workers in those shirt and sneaker factories are, inevitably, paid very little and expected to endure terrible working conditions. I say "inevitably" because their employers are not in business for their (or their workers') health; they will of course try to pay as little as possible, and that minimum is determined by the other opportunities available to workers. And in many cases these are still extremely poor countries.

Yet in those countries where the new export industries took root, there has been unmistakable improvement in the lives of ordi-nary people. Partly this is because a growing industry must offer its workers a somewhat higher wage than they could get elsewhere just in order to get them to move. More important, however, the growth of manufacturing, and of the penumbra of other jobs that the new export sector created, had a ripple effect throughout the economy. The pressure on the land became less intense, so rural wages rose; the pool of unemployed urban dwellers always anxious for work shrank, so factories started to compete with one another for workers, and urban wages also began to rise. In countries where the process has gone on long enough—say, in South Korea or Taiwan—wages have reached advanced-country levels. (In 1975 the average hourly wage in South Korea was only 5 percent of that in the United States; by 2006 it had risen to 62 percent.)

The benefits of export-led economic growth to the mass of people in the newly industrializing economies were not a matter of conjecture. A place like Indonesia is still so poor that progress can be measured in terms of how much the average person gets to eat; between 1968 and 1990 per capita intake rose from 2,000 to 2,700 calories a day, and life expectancy rose from forty-six years to sixty-three. Similar improvements could be seen throughout the Pacific Rim, and even in places like Bangladesh. These improvements did not take place because well-meaning people in the West did anything to help—foreign aid, never large, shrank in the 1990s to virtually nothing. Nor was it the result of the benign policies of national governments, which, as we were soon to be forcefully reminded, were as callous and corrupt as ever. It was the indirect and unintended result of the actions of soulless multinational corporations and rapacious local entrepreneurs, whose only concern was to take advantage of the profit opportunities offered by cheap labor. It was not an edifying spectacle; but no matter how base the motives of those involved, the result was to move hundreds of millions of people from abject poverty to something that was in some cases still awful but nonetheless significantly better.

And once again, capitalism could with considerable justification claim the credit. Socialists had long promised development; there was a time when the Third World looked to Stalin's five-year plans as the very image of how a backward nation should push itself into the twentieth century. And even after the Soviet Union had lost its aura of progressiveness, many intellectuals believed that only by cutting themselves off from competition with more advanced economies could poor nations hope to break out of their trap. By the 1990s, however, there were role models showing that rapid development was possible after all—and it had been accomplished not through proud socialist isolation but precisely by becoming as integrated as possible with global capitalism.

Skeptics and Critics

Not everyone was happy with the state of the world economy after the fall of Communism. While the United States was experiencing remarkable prosperity, other advanced economies were more troubled. Japan had never recovered from the bursting of its "bubble economy" at the beginning of the 1990s, and Europe still suffered from "Eurosclerosis," the persistence of high unemployment rates, especially among the young, even during economic recoveries.

Nor did everyone in the United States share in the general prosperity. The benefits of growth were unequally shared: inequality of both wealth and income had increased to levels not seen since the Great Gatsby days, and by official measures real wages had actually declined for many workers. Even if the numbers were taken with a grain of salt, it was pretty clear that the American economy's progress had left at least 20 or 30 million people at the bottom of the distribution slipping backward.

Some people found other things to be outraged about. The low wages and poor working conditions in those Third World export industries were a frequent source of moralizing—after all, by First World standards those workers were certainly miserable, and these critics had little patience with the argument that bad jobs at bad wages are better than no jobs at all. More justifiably, humanitarians pointed out that large parts of the world were completely untouched by the benefits of globalization: Africa, in particular, was still a continent of ever-deepening poverty, spreading disease, and brutal conflict.

And as always, there were doomsayers. But ever since the 1930s there have been people predicting a new depression any day now; sensible observers have learned not to take such warnings seriously. And that's why ominous developments in Latin America during the first half of the 1990s—developments that did, we now know, signal the possibility of a return to depression economics— were generally ignored.

2

WARNING IGNORED:
LATIN AMERICA'S CRISES

Imagine playing word association—in which one person says a word or phrase, and the other is supposed to reply with the first thing that pops into his mind—with an experienced international banker, finance official, or economist. Until very recently, and perhaps even now, if you said, "Financial crisis," he would surely reply, "Latin America."

For generations, Latin American countries were almost uniquely subject to currency crises, banking failures, bouts of hyperinflation, and all the other monetary ills known to modern man. Weak elected governments alternated with military strongmen, both trying to buy popular support with populist programs they could not afford. In the effort to finance these programs, governments resorted either to borrowing from careless foreign bankers, with the end result being balance-of-payments crisis and default, or to the printing press, with the end result being hyperinflation. To this day, when economists tell parables about the dangers of "macroeconomic populism," about the many ways in which money can go bad, the hypothetical currency is by convention named the "peso."

But by the late 1980s it seemed that Latin America had finally learned its lesson. Few Latins admired the brutality of Augusto Pinochet; but the economic reforms he launched in Chile proved highly successful and were preserved intact when Chile finally returned to democracy in 1989. Chile's return to the Victorian virtues—to sound money and free markets—began to look increasingly attractive as the country's growth rate accelerated. Moreover, the old policies seemed finally to have reached the end of the road: the Latin American debt crisis that began in 1982 dragged on for most of the decade, and it became increasingly clear that only some radical change in policy would get the region moving again.

And so Latin America reformed. State-owned companies were privatized, restrictions on imports lifted, budget deficits trimmed. Controlling inflation became a priority; as we will see, some countries adopted drastic measures to restore confidence in their currencies. And these efforts were quickly rewarded not only with greater efficiency but also in the renewed confidence of foreign investors. Countries that had spent the 1980s as financial pariahs—as late as 1990, creditors who wanted out of Latin debt and sold their claims to less risk-averse investors received, on average, only thirty cents on the dollar—became darlings of the international markets, receiving inflows of money that dwarfed the bank loans that got them into the original debt crisis. International media began to talk about the "new" Latin America, in particular about the "Mexican miracle." In September 1994 the annual World Competitiveness Report, prepared by the people who run the famous Davos conferences, featured a special message from the hero of the hour, the Mexican president, Carlos Salinas.

Three months later, Mexico plunged into its worst financial crisis yet. The so-called tequila crisis caused one of the worst recessions to hit an individual country since the 1930s. The repercussions of that crisis spread across Latin America, coming perilously close to bringing down Argentina's banking system. In retrospect, the tequila crisis should have been seen as an omen, a warning that the good opinion of the markets can be fickle, that today's good press does not insulate you from tomorrow's crisis of confidence.

But the warning was ignored. To understand why, we need to look at the strangely ignored story of Latin America's great crisis.

Mexico: Up from the 1980s

Nobody could describe Mexico's government as unsophisticated. The president's inner circle, the so-called Científicos, were well-educated young men who wanted Mexico to become a modern nation and believed that this required close integration with the world economy. Foreign investors were welcomed, their property rights assured. And, impressed with the progressive leadership, such investors came in large numbers, playing a crucial role in the country's modernization.

Okay, I've just played a trick on you. I'm not describing a recent Mexican government. I'm describing the regime of Porfirio Díaz, who ruled Mexico from 1876 until his regime was overthrown by a popular uprising in 1911. The stable government that emerged after the ensuing decade of civil war was populist, nationalist, suspicious of foreign investors in general and the United States in particular. Members of the new regime, the wonderfully named Institutional Revolutionary Party, or PRI, wanted to modernize Mexico, but they wanted to do it their way: industries were developed by domestic companies to serve the domestic market, sheltered from more efficient foreigners by tariffs and import restrictions. Foreign money was acceptable, as long as it did not bring foreign control; the Mexican government was happy to let its companies borrow from U.S. banks, as long as the voting shares remained in local hands.

This inward-looking economic policy may have been inefficient; aside from the *maquiladoras*, export-oriented factories that were allowed to operate only in a narrow zone near the U.S. border, Mexico failed to take advantage of the rising tide of globalization. But once established, Mexico's development policy became deeply entrenched in the country's political and social system, defended by an iron triangle of industrial oligarchs (who received preferential access to credit and import licenses), politicians (who received largesse from the oligarchs), and labor unions (which represented a "labor aristocracy" of relatively well-paid workers in the sheltered industries). Until the 1970s, it must also be said, Mexico was careful not to overreach financially; growth was disappointing, but there were no crises.

In the late 1970s, however, that traditional caution was thrown to the winds. The Mexican economy entered a feverish boom, fed by new oil discoveries, high prices for that oil, and large loans from foreign banks. As the economy heated up and money came rolling in, few people saw the warning signs. There were scattered press stories suggesting some emerging financial problems, but the general view was that Mexico (and Latin America in general) posed few financial risks. This complacency can be quantified: as late as July 1982 the yield on Mexican bonds was slightly *less* than that on those of presumably safe borrowers like the World Bank, indicating that investors regarded the risk that Mexico would fail to pay on time as negligible.

In the middle of the next month, however, a delegation of Mexican officials flew to Washington to inform the U.S. treasury secretary that they were out of money and that Mexico could no longer honor its debts. Within a few months the crisis had spread through most of Latin America and beyond, as banks stopped lending and began demanding repayment. Through frantic efforts—emergency loans from the U.S. government and international agencies like the Bank for International Settlements, "rescheduling" of loan repayments, and what was politely known as "concerted lending" (in which banks were more or less coerced into lending countries the money they needed to pay interest on outstanding loans)—most countries managed to avoid an outright default. The price of this narrow avoidance of financial catastrophe, however, was a severe recession, followed by a slow and often sputtering recovery. By 1986 Mexican real income per capita was 10 percent lower than it had been in 1981, and real wages, eroded by an average inflation rate of more than 70 percent over the preceding four years, were 30 percent below their pre-crisis level.

Enter the new generation of reformers. Over the course of the 1970s a "new class" had become increasingly influential within Mexico's ruling party and government. Well educated, often with graduate degrees from Harvard or MIT, fluent in English and internationalist in outlook, they were Mexican enough to navigate the PRI's boss-and-patronage political waters, but Americanized enough to believe that things should be different. The economic crisis left the old guard, the "dinosaurs," at a loss for answers; the "technopols," who could explain how free-market reforms had worked in Chile, how export-oriented growth had worked in Korea, how inflation stabilization had been achieved in Israel, found themselves the men of the hour. They were not alone: by the mid-1980s many Latin American economists had abandoned the statist views of the fifties and sixties in favor of what came to be called the

Washington Consensus: growth could best be achieved via sound budgets, low inflation, deregulated markets, and free trade.

In 1985 President Miguel de la Madrid began to put this doctrine into effect, most dramatically through a radical freeing up of Mexico's trade: tariffs were slashed, and the range of imports requiring government licenses drastically reduced. The government began selling off some of the enterprises it owned, and loosened the strict rules governing foreign ownership. Perhaps most remarkable of all, de la Madrid designated as his successor not one of the usual PRI bosses but a champion of the new reformers: Planning and Budget Secretary Carlos Salinas de Gortari, himself possessed of a degree from Harvard's Kennedy School of Government, and surrounded by a staff of highly regarded economists trained mainly at MIT.

I use the phrase "designated as his successor" advisedly. Mexico's political system from 1920 to 1990 was truly unique. On paper it was a representative democracy; in recent years that piece of fiction has, amazingly, started to become reality. But in 1988, the year Salinas was elected, Mexican democracy was really a sort of souped-up version of traditional Chicago politics: a one-party system in which votes were bought through patronage, and any shortfall was made up through creative vote counting. The remarkable thing about this system, however, was that the president himself, while very nearly an absolute monarch during his six-year term, could not seek a second term; he would step down, somehow having become wealthy during his tenure, and hand over the reins to a designated successor who would be nominated by the PRI and inevitably win.

By 1988 this system, like Mexico as a whole, was under strain. Salinas faced a real challenger in the general election: Cuauhtémoc Cárdenas, son of a popular former president, who countered Salinas's free-market reformism with a more traditional, anti-capitalist populism. It was a close election, and Cárdenas won. But that was not how the official tally came out. Salinas became president, but now, more than any of his predecessors, he had to deliver the goods. For that, he turned to his Cambridge-trained economic team.

The successes of the Salinas years were built on two crucial policy moves. First was a resolution of the debt crisis. In early 1989, its own presidential election safely past, the U.S. government began showing some unexpected willingness to face up to unpleasant realities. It finally admitted what everyone had long known, that many savings and loan associations had been gambling with taxpayer money and needed to be shut down. Meanwhile, in a surprise speech, Treasury Secretary Nicholas Brady declared that Latin America's debt could not be fully repaid and that some kind of debt forgiveness would have to be worked out. The so-called Brady Plan was more a sentiment than an actual plan—Brady's speech emerged from bureaucratic intrigues worthy of *Yes, Minister*, during which those government officials who might have had the technical expertise to put together a workable blueprint for debt relief were kept in the dark, for fear that they might raise objections. But it gave the extremely competent Mexicans the opening they needed. Within a few months they had devised a scheme that was workable. Mexico ended up replacing much of its outstanding debt with a smaller face value of "Brady bonds."

The overall debt relief from Mexico's Brady deal was modest, but it represented a psychological turning point. Mexicans who had long agitated for debt repudiation were mollified by seeing the foreign bankers give up a pound of flesh; the debt faded as a domestic political issue. Meanwhile foreign investors, who had been afraid to put funds into Mexico for fear that they would be trapped there, saw the deal as putting a period to that phase, and became ready to put in fresh money. The interest rates that Mexico had been forced to pay to keep money from fleeing the country plunged; and because the government no longer had to pay such high interest rates on its debt, the budget deficit quickly faded away. Within a year after the Brady deal, Mexico's financial situation had been transformed.

Nor was a resolution of the debt problem the only trick up Salinas's sleeve. In 1990 he astonished the world by proposing that Mexico establish free trade with the United States and Canada (which had already negotiated a free-trade agreement with each other). In quantitative terms the proposed North American Free Trade Agreement, or NAFTA, would matter less than one might have thought: the U.S. market was already fairly open to Mexican products, and the trade liberalization begun by de la Madrid had moved Mexico itself much, though not all, of the way to free trade. But like the debt reduction package, NAFTA was intended to mark a psychological turning point. By making Mexico's moves to open up to foreign goods and foreign investors not merely a domestic initiative but part of an international treaty, Salinas hoped to make those moves irreversible—and to convince the markets that they were irreversible. He also hoped to guarantee that Mexico's opening would be reciprocated, that the United States would in effect assure Mexico of access to its own market in perpetuity.

George H. W. Bush accepted Salinas's offer. How could he refuse? When the Mexican debt crisis struck in 1982, many in the United States feared that it would lead to a radicalization of Mexican politics, that anti-American forces—perhaps even Communists—would rise in the resulting chaos. Instead, pro-American, free-market types—our kind of people—had miraculously come to power, and offered to take down all the old barriers. To turn them down would be a slap in the face for reform; it would be practically to invite instability and hostility in our neighbor. On compelling foreign-policy grounds, then, American diplomats were enthusiastic about NAFTA. Convincing Congress turned out to be a bit harder, as we will see. But in the first flush of enthusiasm, that was not yet apparent.

Instead, as the reforms in Mexico continued—as state enterprises were sold off, more import restrictions lifted, foreign investors welcomed—enthusiasm for Mexico's prospects accelerated. I personally recall talking to a group of multinational executives—heads of their companies' Latin American operations—in Cancún back in March 1993. I expressed some mild reservations about the Mexican situation, some evidence that the payoff to reform was a bit disappointing. "You're the only person in this room with anything negative to say about this country," I was politely informed. And people like those in the room put their money where their mouths were: in 1993 more than $30 billion in foreign capital was invested in Mexico.

Argentina's Break with the Past

"Rich as an Argentine." That was a common epithet in Europe before World War I, a time when Argentina was viewed by the public, and by investors, as a land of opportunity. Like Australia, Canada, and the United States, Argentina was a resource-rich nation, a favorite destination for both European emigrants and European capital. Buenos Aires was a gracious city with a European feel, hub of a first-rate British-built and -financed railway network, which gathered the wheat and meat of the pampas for export to the world. Linked by trade and investment to the global economy, by telegraph cable to the world capital market, Argentina was a member in good standing of the prewar international system.

True, even then Argentina had a certain tendency now and then to print too much money and to get into difficulties servicing its foreign debt. But then so did the United States. Few could have imagined that Argentina would eventually fall so far behind.

The interwar years were difficult for Argentina, as they were for all resource-exporting countries. The prices of agricultural products were low in the 1920s and crashed in the 1930s. And the situation was made worse by the debt run up in happier years. In effect, Argentina was like a farmer who borrowed heavily when times were good, and finds himself painfully squeezed between falling prices and fixed loan payments. Still, Argentina did not do as badly as one might have expected during the Depression. Its government proved less doctrinaire than those of advanced countries determined to defend the monetary proprieties at all costs. Thanks to a devalued peso, controls on capital flight, and a moratorium on debt repayment, Argentina was actually able to achieve a reasonably strong recovery after 1932; indeed, by 1934 Europeans were once again emigrating to Argentina, because they had a better prospect of finding jobs there than at home.

But the success of heterodox policies during the Depression helped establish governing habits that proved increasingly destructive as time went by. Emergency controls on foreign exchange became a nightmarishly complex set of regulations that discouraged enterprise and fostered corruption. Temporary limitations on imports became permanent barriers behind which astonishingly inefficient industries survived. Nationalized enterprises became sinks for public funds, employing hundreds of thousands of people yet failing to deliver essential services. And deficit spending repeatedly ran amok, leading to ever more disruptive bouts of inflation.

In the 1980s things went from bad to worse. After the debacle of the Falklands War in 1982, Argentina's military government had stepped down, and the civilian government of Raúl Alfonsín took power with the promise of economic revitalization. But the Latin American debt crisis struck Argentina as hard as the rest of the region, and Alfonsín's attempt to stabilize prices by introducing a new currency, the austral, failed dismally. By 1989 the nation was suffering from true hyperinflation, with prices rising at an annual rate of 3,000 percent.

The victor in the 1989 election was Carlos Menem, the Peronist —that is, the candidate of the party founded by Juan Perón, whose nationalistic and protectionist policies had done more than any-thing else to turn Argentina into a Third World nation. But Menem, it turned out, was prepared to do an economic version of Nixon's trip to China. As finance minister he appointed Domingo Cavallo, a Ph.D. from Harvard (of the same vintage as Pedro Aspe, Mexi-co's finance minister during the lead-up to its crisis); and Cavallo devised a reform plan even more radical than that of Mexico.

Part of the plan involved opening Argentina up to world markets —in particular, ending the long-standing, destructive habit of treat-ing the country's agricultural exports as a cash cow, to be taxed at prohibitive rates in order to subsidize everything else. Privatiza-tion of the country's immense and utterly inefficient state-owned sector also proceeded at a rapid clip. (Unlike Mexico, Argentina even privatized the state-owned oil company.) Because Argentina's initial policies were arguably among the worst in the world, these reforms made a huge difference.

But the distinctive Cavallo touch was the monetary reform. In order to put a definitive end to the country's history of inflation, he resurrected a monetary system that had almost been forgotten in the modern world: a currency board.

Currency boards used to be standard in European colonial possessions. Such possessions would ordinarily be allowed to issue their own currency; but the currency would be rigidly tied in value to that of the mother country, and its soundness would be guaranteed by a law requiring that the domestic currency issue be fully backed by hard-currency reserves. That is, the public would be entitled to convert local currency into pounds or francs at a legally fixed rate, and the central bank would be obliged to keep enough of the mother country's currency on hand to exchange for all of the local notes.

In the postwar years, with the decline of colonial empires and the rise of active economic management, currency boards faded into oblivion. True, in 1983 Hong Kong, faced with a run on its currency, instituted a currency board pegging the Hong Kong dollar at 7.8 to the U.S. dollar. But Hong Kong was itself a sort of colonial relic, albeit a remarkably dynamic one, and the precedent attracted only limited attention.

Argentina's need for credibility, however, was desperate, and so Cavallo reached into the past. The ill-starred austral was replaced with a born-again peso, and this new peso was set at a permanently fixed exchange rate of one peso, one dollar—with every peso in circulation backed by a dollar of reserves. After decades of abusing its money, Argentina had, by law, renounced the ability to print money at all unless someone wanted to exchange a dollar for a peso.

The results were impressive. Inflation dropped rapidly to near zero. Like Mexico, Argentina negotiated a Brady deal and was rewarded with a resumption of capital inflow, though not on the same scale. And the real economy perked up dramatically: after years of decline, GDP increased by a quarter in just three years.

Mexico's Bad Year

At the end of 1993, were there any clouds on Latin America's horizon? Investors were euphoric: it seemed to them that the new free-market orientation of the continent had turned it into a land of opportunity. Foreign businessmen, like those I talked to in Cancún, were almost equally upbeat: the newly liberalized environment had created vast new opportunities for them. Only a few economists had questions, and these were relatively mild.

One question common to both Mexico and Argentina was the appropriateness of the exchange rate. Both countries had stabilized their currencies; both had brought inflation down; but in both cases the slowdown in inflation lagged behind the stabilization of the exchange rate. In Argentina, for example, the peso was pegged against the dollar in 1991; yet over the next two years consumer prices rose 40 percent, compared with only 6 in the United States. A similar, if less stark, process occurred in Mexico. In both cases the effect was to make the country's goods expensive on world markets, leading economists to wonder if their currencies had become overvalued.

A related question involved the trade balance (more accurately, the current account balance, a broader measure that includes services, payment of interest, and so on—but I will use the terms interchangeably). In the early 1990s Mexico's exports grew rather slowly, mainly because the strong peso made their prices uncompetitive. At the same time imports, pulled in both by the removal of import barriers and by a boom in credit, surged. The result was a huge excess of imports over exports: by 1993 Mexico's deficit had reached 8 percent of GDP, a number with few historical precedents. Was this a sign of trouble?

Mexican officials, and many outside the country, argued that

it was not. Their argument came straight out of economics textbooks. As a sheer matter of accounting, the balance of payments
always balances: that is, every purchase that a country makes from
foreigners must be matched by a sale of equal value. (Economics
students know that there is a small technical qualification to this
statement involving unrequited transfers; never mind.) If a country is running a deficit on its *current* account—buying more goods
than it sells—it must correspondingly be running an equal surplus
on its *capital* account—selling more *assets* than it buys. And the
converse is equally true: a country that runs a surplus on capital
account must run a deficit on current account. But that meant that
Mexico's success in getting foreigners to bring their money, to buy
Mexican assets, had a trade deficit as its necessary counterpart—
the deficit, in fact, was simply another way of saying that foreigners
thought Mexico was a great place to invest. The only reason to be
concerned, said the optimists, would be if the capital inflow were
somehow artificial—if the government were pulling capital in from
abroad by borrowing the money itself (as it did before 1982) or by
running budget deficits that created a shortage of domestic savings. Mexico's government, however, was running a balanced budget and was actually building up overseas assets (foreign exchange
reserves) rather than liabilities. So why be concerned? If the private
sector wanted to pour capital into Mexico, why should the government try to stop it?

And yet there was a disturbing aspect of Mexico's performance:
given all the reforms, and all that capital coming in, where was
the growth?

Between 1981 and 1989 the Mexican economy had grown at an
annual rate of only 1.3 percent, well short of population growth,
leaving per capita income far below its 1981 peak. From 1990 to
1994, the years of the "Mexican miracle," things were definitely

better: the economy grew 2.8 percent per year. But this was still barely ahead of population growth; as of 1994 Mexico was still, according to its own statistics, far below its 1981 level. Where was the miracle—indeed, where was the payoff to all those reforms, all that foreign investment? In 1993 the MIT economist Rudiger Dornbusch, a longtime observer of the Mexican economy (and the teacher of many of the economists now running Mexico, Aspe included), wrote a caustic analysis of the situation entitled "Mexico: Stabilization, Reform, and No Growth."

Defenders of the Mexican record argued that these numbers failed to reveal the true progress of the economy, especially the transformation from an inefficient, inward-looking industrial base to a highly competitive export orientation. Still, it was certainly disturbing that the huge capital inflows were producing so little measurable result. What was going wrong?

Dornbusch and others argued that the problem lay in the value of the peso: an excessively strong currency was pricing Mexican goods out of world markets, preventing the economy from taking advantage of its growing capacity. What Mexico needed, then, was a devaluation—a onetime reduction in the dollar value of the peso, which would get its economy moving again. After all, in 1992 Britain had been forced by the financial markets (and in particular by George Soros—see Chapter 6) to let the value of the pound decline, and the result was to turn a recession into a boom. Mexico, said some, needed a dose of the same medicine. (Similar arguments were also made for Argentina, whose economy had grown much faster than Mexico's but faced stubbornly high unemployment.)

The Mexicans dismissed such talk, assuring investors that their economic program was on track, that they saw no reason to devalue the peso, and that they had no intention of doing so. It was particularly important to put up a good front because the North American Free Trade Agreement required approval from the U.S. Congress and had run into stiff opposition. Ross Perot had memorably warned of the "great sucking sound" the United States would hear as all its jobs moved south; more respectable voices offered more respectable-sounding arguments. During 1993 the Clinton administration, which had inherited NAFTA from its predecessor, pulled out all the stops and with great difficulty secured passage; but it was a pretty close thing—and just in time.

For during the course of 1994 some important things started to go wrong in Mexico. On New Year's Day there was a peasant uprising in the poor rural state of Chiapas, an area that had gone untouched economically or politically by the changes sweeping through much of Mexico. The stability of the government was not threatened, but the incident was a reminder that bad old habits of corruption, and grinding rural poverty, were still very much a part of the Mexican scene. More serious was the March assassination of Donaldo Colosio, Salinas's designated successor. Colosio was a rare combination of reformer and charismatic popular politician, widely regarded as just the man to truly legitimize the new way of doing things; his assassination both deprived the country of a much needed leader and suggested that dark forces (corrupt political bosses? drug lords?) did not want a strong reformer in charge. The replacement candidate, Ernesto Zedillo, was an American-trained economist whose honesty and intelligence were not in question; but was he a political naïf who would allow himself to be bullied by the dinosaurs? Finally, in the run-up to the election the PRI set about trying to buy support with a moderately large spending spree; some of the pesos it printed were converted into dollars, draining the foreign exchange reserves.

Zedillo won the election, fairly this time, because he managed to convince voters that the populist views of Cárdenas would provoke a financial crisis—as one Mexican friend put it to me, the PRI convinced the voters that unless they voted for Zedillo, "what did happen, would happen." For, alas, the financial crisis came anyway.

The Tequila Crisis

In December 1994, faced with a steady drain on their reserves of foreign exchange, Mexican authorities had to decide what to do. They could stem the loss by raising interest rates, thereby making it attractive for Mexican residents to keep their money in pesos, and perhaps attracting in foreign funds as well. But this rise in interest rates would hurt business and consumer spending, and Mexico was, after several years of disappointing growth, already on the edge of a recession. Or they could devalue the peso—reduce its value in terms of dollars—hoping that this would have the same effect as in Britain sixteen months earlier. That is, a devaluation could in the best scenario not only make Mexico's exports more competitive but also convince foreign investors that Mexican assets were good value, and hence actually allow interest rates to fall.

Mexico chose devaluation. But it botched the job.

What is supposed to happen when a country's currency is devalued is that speculators say, "Okay, that's over," and stop betting on the currency's continued decline. That's the way it worked for Britain and Sweden in 1992. The danger is that speculators will instead view the first devaluation as a sign of more to come, and start speculating all the harder. In order to avoid that, a government is supposed to follow certain rules. First, if you devalue at all, make the devaluation big enough. Otherwise, you will simply set up expectations of more to come. Second, immediately following the devaluation, you must give every signal you can that everything is under control, that you are responsible people who understand the importance of treating investors right, and so on. Otherwise the devaluation can crystallize doubts about your economy's soundness and start a panic.

Mexico broke both rules. The initial devaluation was 15 percent, only half of what economists like Dornbusch had been suggesting. And the behavior of government officials was anything but reassuring. The new finance minister, Jaime Serra Puche, appeared arrogant and indifferent to the opinion of foreign creditors. Worse yet, it soon became clear that some Mexican businessmen had been consulted about the devaluation in advance, giving them inside information denied to foreign investors. Massive capital flight was now inevitable, and the Mexican government soon had to abandon fixing the exchange rate at all.

Still, Serra Puche was quickly replaced, and Mexico began making all the right noises. And one might have thought that all the reforms since 1985 would count for something. But no: foreign investors were shocked—shocked!—to discover that Mexico was not the paragon it had seemed, and wanted out at any cost. Soon the peso had fallen to half its pre-crisis value.

The most pressing problem was the government's own budget. Governments whose financial credibility is suspect have trouble selling long-term bonds and usually end up with substantial amounts of short-term debt that must be rolled over at frequent intervals. Mexico was no exception; and the need to pay high interest rates on that debt was a major source of fiscal problems in the 1980s. As we saw, one of the big benefits of the Brady deal of 1989 was that by making investors more confident, it allowed Mexico to roll over its short-term debt at much reduced interest rates. Now these gains were lost, and more: by March Mexico was paying investors an interest rate of 75 percent.

Worse yet, in an effort to convince the markets that it would not devalue, Mexico had converted billions of short-term debt into so-called *tesobonos*, which were indexed to the dollar. As the peso plunged, the size of these dollarized debts exploded. And as the *tesobono* problem received wide publicity, it only reinforced the sense of panic.

The government's financial crisis soon spilled over into the private sector. During 1995 Mexico's real GDP would plunge 7 percent, its industrial production 15 percent, far worse than anything the United States has seen since the 1930s—indeed, far worse than the initial slump that followed the 1982 debt crisis. Thousands of businesses went bankrupt; hundreds of thousands of workers lost their jobs. Exactly why the financial crisis had such a devastating effect on the real economy—and why the Mexican government could not, baby-sitting co-op style, act to prevent that slump—is a key question. But let us postpone that discussion until we have a few more crises under our belt.

Most startling of all, the crisis was not confined to Mexico. Instead, the "tequila effect" spread across much of the world, and in particular to other Latin America countries, especially Argentina.

This was an unpleasant surprise. For one thing, Argentina and Mexico are at the opposite ends of Latin America, with few direct trade or financial links. Moreover, Argentina's currency board system was supposed to make the credibility of *its* peso invulnerable. How could it be caught up in Mexico's crisis?

Perhaps Argentina was attacked because to Yanqui investors all Latin American nations look alike. But once speculation against the Argentine peso began, it became clear that the currency board did not provide the kind of insulation its creators had hoped for. True, every peso in circulation was backed by a dollar in reserves, so that in a mechanical sense the country could always defend the peso's value. But what would happen when the public, rationally or not, began to change large numbers of pesos into dollars? The answer, it turned out, was that the country's banks moved quickly to the edge of collapse and threatened to bring the rest of the economy down with them.

Here's how it worked: suppose that a New York loan officer, made nervous by the news from Mexico, decides that he had better reduce his Latin American exposure—and that it is not worth trying to explain to his boss that, as Ronald Reagan once remarked, "they're all different countries." So he tells an Argentine client that his credit line will not be renewed and that the outstanding balance must be repaid. The client withdraws the necessary pesos from his local bank, converting them into dollars with no trouble, because the central bank has plenty of dollars on hand. But the Argentine bank must now replenish its cash reserves; so it calls in a loan to an Argentine businessman.

That's where the trouble starts. To repay its loan, the business must acquire pesos, which will probably be withdrawn from an account at some other Argentine bank—which will itself therefore have to call in some loans, leading to more bank withdrawals, leading to further reductions in credit. The initial reduction in lending from abroad, in other words, will have a *multiplied* effect within Argentina: each dollar of reduced credit from New York leads to several pesos of called loans in Buenos Aires.

And as credit contracts, the business situation in Argentina starts to become dicey. Businesses have trouble repaying their loans on short notice, all the more so because their customers are also under financial pressure. Depositors start to wonder whether banks can really collect from their clients, and start to pull their money out just in case, further tightening credit conditions . . . and we have the beginnings of the sort of vicious circle of credit crunch and bank run that devastated the U.S. economy in 1930–31.

Now, modern nations have defenses against that sort of thing. First of all, deposits are insured by the government, so depositors are not supposed to worry about the solvency of their bank. Second, the central bank is prepared to act as "lender of last resort," rushing cash to banks so they aren't forced into desperate fire-sale methods to meet the demands of depositors. Argentina should thus have been able to nip this process in the bud.

But things weren't that easy. Argentine depositors may have believed that their pesos were safe, but they were less sure that they would preserve their value in dollars. So they wanted to make sure by getting into dollars now, just in case. And the central bank couldn't act as lender of last resort because it was prohibited from printing new pesos except in exchange for dollars! The very rules designed to protect the system from one kind of crisis of confidence left it deeply vulnerable to another.

In early 1995, then, both Mexico and Argentina went suddenly from euphoria to terror. It seemed all too likely that the reformist experiments in both countries would end in disastrous collapse.

The Great Rescue

What Latin America needed, urgently, was dollars: dollars with which Mexico could repay the *tesobonos* as they came due, dollars that would allow Argentina to print pesos and lend them to its banks.

The Mexican package was the larger, more urgent, and politically more difficult of the two. While much of the money came from international agencies like the International Monetary Fund, Europe and Japan saw a Mexican rescue as mainly a U.S. issue, and the United States therefore would have to provide a large chunk of the money itself. Unfortunately, there were powerful political forces arrayed against any such rescue. Those who had bitterly opposed NAFTA saw the Mexican crisis as vindication and were not willing to lay out taxpayers' money on behalf of the Mexicans and their bankers. Meanwhile, conservatives disliked the whole idea of governments intervening to support markets, and particularly disliked the role of the International Monetary Fund, which they regarded as a step on the way toward world government. It soon became clear that the U.S. Congress would not approve any funding for a Mexican rescue.

Luckily, it turned out that the U.S. Treasury can, at its own discretion, make use of the Exchange Stabilization Fund (ESF), a pot of money set aside for emergency intervention in foreign exchange markets. The intent of the legislation that established that fund was clearly to stabilize the value of the *dollar*; but the language didn't actually say that. So with admirable creativity Treasury used it to stabilize the peso instead. Between the ESF and other sources, a remarkable $50 billion credit line was quickly made available to Mexico; and after several heart-pounding months the financial situation did indeed begin to stabilize.

Argentina's lower-profile rescue came via the World Bank, which put up $12 billion to support the nation's banks.

The rescues for Mexico and Argentina did not prevent a very severe economic contraction—it was considerably worse, in fact, than what happened in the first year of the 1980s debt crisis. But by late 1995 investors began to calm down, to believe that maybe the countries were not going to collapse after all. Interest rates came down; spending started to revive; and soon Mexico and Argentina were making a rapid recovery. For thousands of businesses and millions of workers, the crisis had been devastating. But it ended sooner than most had feared or expected.

Learning the Wrong Lessons

Two years after the tequila crisis, it seemed as if everything was back on track. Both Mexico and Argentina were booming, and those investors who had kept their nerve did very well indeed. And so, perversely, what might have been seen as a warning instead became, if anything, a source of complacency. While few people laid out the lessons learned from the Latin crisis explicitly, an informal summary of the post-tequila conventional wisdom might have run as follows:

First, the tequila crisis was not about the way the world at large works: it was a case of Mexico being Mexico. It was caused by Mexican policy errors—notably, allowing the currency to become overvalued, expanding credit instead of tightening it when speculation against the peso began, and botching the devaluation itself in a way that unnerved investors. And the depth of the slump that followed had mainly to do with the uniquely tricky political economy of the Mexican situation, with its still-unresolved legacy of populism and anti-Americanism. In a way you could say that the slump was punishment for the theft of the 1988 election.

The lesson taken, in short, was that Mexico's debacle was of little relevance to the rest of the world. True, the crisis had spilled over to the rest of Latin America, but Argentina's brush with financial collapse somehow did not fully register on the world's attention, perhaps because it was followed by such a strong recovery. And surely the tequila crisis would not be replicated in well-run econo-mies without a history of macroeconomic populism—countries like the miracle economies of Asia.

The other lesson concerned not Mexico but Washington—that is, the International Monetary Fund and the U.S. Treasury Depart-ment. What the crisis seemed to show was that Washington had things under control: that it had the resources and the knowledge to contain even severe financial crises. Huge aid was quickly mobi-lized on Mexico's behalf, and it did the trick. Instead of the seven lean years of the 1980s, the tequila crisis was over in a year and a half. Clearly, it seemed, the people in charge had gotten better at this sort of thing.

Fourteen years after the tequila crisis began, with much of the world, including the United States, experiencing a financial crisis with a distinct resemblance to the events of 1994–95, it's clear that we learned the wrong lessons from Latin America.

What we should have asked was the question posed in many meetings by the economist Guillermo Calvo, of the World Bank and later of the University of Maryland: "Why was so large a pun-ishment imposed for so small a crime?" In the aftermath of the tequila crisis it was all too easy to revisit the policies followed by Mexico in the run-up to that crisis, and find them full of error. But the fact was that at the time they seemed pretty good, and even after the fact it was hard to find any missteps large enough to justify the economic catastrophe of 1995. We should have taken Calvo's question—with its implication that there were mechanisms trans-forming minor policy mistakes into major economic disasters—to heart. We should have looked more closely at the arguments of some commentators that there really were no serious mistakes at all, except for the brief series of fumbles that got Mexico on the wrong side of market perceptions and set in motion a process of self-justifying panic. And we should therefore also have realized that what happened to Mexico could happen elsewhere: that the seeming success of an economy, the admiration of markets and media for its managers, was no guarantee that the economy was immune to sudden financial crisis.

In retrospect it is also clear that we gave far too much credit to "Washington," to the IMF and the Treasury. It was true that they had acted courageously and decisively, and that the results had been a vindication. But on close examination the omens were not all that good for a repeat performance. For one thing, the mobilization of money was achieved through what amounted to a legal sleight of hand, justified mainly by the special significance of Mexico to U.S. interests. Money would not come as quickly or as easily in later crises. The Mexican rescue was also made less complicated by the cooperation of the Mexican government: Zedillo's people had no pride to swallow—not with Mexico's history—and were in complete agreement with Washington about what needed to be done. Dealing with Asian countries that had been accustomed to negotiating from a position of strength, and with Asian leaders accustomed to having things their own way, would be very different.

Perhaps most of all, we failed to understand the extent to which both Mexico and Washington simply got lucky. The rescue wasn't really a well-considered plan that addressed the essence of the crisis: it was an emergency injection of cash to a beleaguered government, which did its part by adopting painful measures less because they were clearly related to the economic problems than because by demonstrating the government's seriousness they might restore market confidence. They succeeded, albeit only after the economy had been punished severely, but there was no good reason to suppose that such a strategy would work the next time.

And so nobody was prepared either for the emergence of a new, tequila-style crisis in Asia a few years later, or for the ineffectiveness of a Mexican-style rescue when that crisis came. We were even less prepared for the global crisis that erupted in 2007. What was odd about our obliviousness was that Asia's biggest economy was already in serious trouble—and was doing a notably bad job taking care of its own business.

3

JAPAN'S TRAP

There was a time, not that long ago, when Americans were obsessed with Japan. The successes of Japanese industry inspired both admiration and fear; you couldn't enter an airport bookstore without encountering rows of dust jackets featuring rising suns and samurai warriors. Some of these books promised to teach the secrets of Japanese management; others prophesied (or demanded) economic warfare. As role models or demons, or both, the Japanese were very much on our minds.

All that is gone now. Japan still makes the headlines now and then, usually when there's bad news—a big fall in the Nikkei, or a disruption of the "carry trade," in which hedge funds borrow cheaply in Japan and lend the money elsewhere. But for the most part we have lost interest. The Japanese weren't that tough after all, the public seems to have concluded, so now we can ignore them.

This is foolish. The failures of Japan are every bit as significant for us as its successes. What happened to Japan is both a tragedy and an omen. The world's second-largest economy is still blessed with well-educated and willing workers, a modern capital stock, and impressive technological know-how. It has a stable government, which has no difficulty collecting taxes. Unlike Latin America, or for that matter smaller Asian economies, it is a creditor nation, not dependent on the goodwill of foreign investors. And the sheer size of its economy, which means that its producers sell mainly to the domestic market, should give Japan—like the United States—a freedom of action denied to lesser nations.

Yet Japan spent most of the 1990s in a slump, alternating brief and inadequate periods of economic growth with ever-deeper recessions. Once the growth champion of the advanced world, in 1998 Japanese industry produced less than it had in 1991. And even worse than the performance itself was the sense of fatalism and helplessness, the loss of faith in the ability of public policy to turn the situation around. This was a tragedy: a great economy like this does not need or deserve to be in a decade-long slump. Japan's woes were never as acute as those of other Asian nations, but they went on far longer, with far less justification. It was also an omen: if it could happen to the Japanese, who was to say that it couldn't happen to us? And sure enough, it did.

How did it happen to Japan?

Japan as Number One

No country—not even the Soviet Union in the days of Stalin's five-year plans—had ever experienced as stunning an economic transformation as Japan did in the high-growth years from 1953 to 1973. In the space of two decades a largely agricultural nation became the world's largest exporter of steel and automobiles, greater Tokyo became the world's largest and arguably most vibrant metropolitan area, and the standard of living made a quantum leap.

Some Westerners took notice. As early as 1969 the futurist Herman Kahn published *The Emerging Japanese Superstate*, predicting that Japan's high growth rates would make it the world's leading economy by the year 2000. But it was not until the late 1970s—around the time that Ezra Vogel wrote his best-seller, *Japan as Number One*—that the realization of just how much Japan had achieved really dawned on the wider public. As sophisticated Japanese products—above all, automobiles and consumer electronics—flooded into Western markets, people began to wonder about the secret of Japan's success.

There was a certain irony in the timing of the great debate about Japan: the truth was that the heroic age of Japanese economic growth ended just about the time Westerners started to take Japan seriously. In the early 1970s, for reasons that are still somewhat mysterious, growth slowed throughout the advanced world. Japan, which had had the highest growth rate, also experienced the biggest slowdown—from 9 percent a year in the 1960s to less than 4 percent after 1973. Although this rate was still faster than that of any other advanced country (half again as fast as that of the United States), at that rate the date of Japan's emergence as the world's leading economy would have to be put off well into the twenty-first century. Still, Japan's growth performance was, literally, the envy of other nations. Many people argued not only that Japan had figured out a better way to run its economy but also that its success came at least partly at the expense of naive Western competitors.

We need not replay here the whole debate over why Japan was successful. Basically, there were two sides. One side explained the growth as the product of good fundamentals, above all excellent basic education and a high savings rate, and—as always—also engaged in a bit of amateur sociology to explain why Japan was so very good at manufacturing high-quality products at low cost. The other side argued that Japan had developed a fundamentally different economic system, a new and superior form of capitalism. The debate over Japan also became a debate over economic philosophy, over the validity of Western economic thought in general and the virtues of free markets in particular.

One element of the supposedly superior Japanese system was government guidance. In the fifties and sixties the Japanese government—both the famed Ministry of International Trade and Industry (MITI) and the quieter but even more influential Ministry of Finance—played a strong role in directing the economy. The economy's growth was at least partly channeled by the government's strategic designs, as bank loans and import licenses flowed to favored industries and firms. By the time the West really focused on Japan, the government's grip had been much loosened, but the image of "Japan Inc.," a centrally directed economy bent on dominating world markets, remained a potent one into the 1990s.

Another element of the distinctive Japanese economic style was the insulation of major companies from short-term financial pressures. Members of Japanese *keiretsu*—groups of allied firms organized around a main bank—typically owned substantial quantities of each other's shares, making management largely independent of the outside stockholders. Nor did Japanese companies worry much about stock prices, or market confidence, since they rarely financed themselves by selling either stocks or bonds. Instead, the main bank lent them the money they needed. So Japanese firms didn't have to worry about short-term profitability, or indeed to worry much about profitability at all. One might have thought that the financial condition of a *keiretsu* bank would in the end discipline corporate investment: if the loans to the bank's affiliates looked unsound, wouldn't the bank start to lose depositors? But in Japan as in most countries, depositors believed that the government would never allow them to lose their savings, so they paid little attention to what banks did with their money.

The result of this system, claimed both those who admired it and those who feared it, was a country able to take the long view. One by one, the Japanese government would target "strategic" industries that could serve as engines of growth. The private sector would be guided into those industries, helped along by an initial period of protection from foreign competition, during which the industry could hone its skills in the domestic market. Then there would be a great export drive, during which firms would ignore profitability while building market share and driving their foreign competitors into the ground. Eventually, its dominance of the industry secured, Japan would move on to the next one. Steel, autos, VCRs, semiconductors—soon it would be computers and aircraft.

Skeptics poked holes in many of the details of this account. But even those who absolved Japan of the charge of predatory behavior, who questioned whether the wizards of MITI were really as all-knowing as advertised, tended to agree that the distinctive characteristics of the Japanese system must have something to do with Japanese success. Only much later would those same distinctive characteristics—the cozy relationship between government and business, the extension of easy credit by government-guaranteed banks to closely allied companies—come to be labeled crony capitalism and seen as the root of economic malaise.

But the weaknesses of the system were actually evident by the late 1980s, to anyone willing to see.

Bubble, Toil and Trouble

At the beginning of 1990 the market capitalization of Japan—the total value of all the stocks of all the nation's companies—was larger than that of the United States, which had twice Japan's population and more than twice its gross domestic product. Land, never cheap in crowded Japan, had become incredibly expensive: according to a widely cited factoid, the land underneath the square mile of Tokyo's Imperial Palace was worth more than the entire state of California. Welcome to the "bubble economy," Japan's equivalent of the Roaring Twenties.

The late 1980s represented a time of prosperity for Japan, of fast growth, low unemployment, and high profits. Nonetheless, nothing in the underlying economic data justified the tripling of both land and stock prices during that period. Even at the time many observers thought that there was something manic and irrational about the financial boom—that traditional companies in slowly growing industries should not be valued like growth stocks, with price-earnings ratios of 60 or more. But as is so often the case in manic markets, the skeptics were without the resources, or the courage, to back their lack of conviction; conventional wisdom found all sorts of justifications for the sky-high prices.

Financial bubbles are nothing new. From tulip mania to Internet mania, even the most sensible investors have found it hard to resist getting caught up in the momentum, to take a long view when everyone else is getting rich. But given the reputation of the Japanese for long-term strategic thinking, the common perception that Japan Inc. was more like a planned economy than a free-market free-for-all, the extent of the bubble remains somewhat surprising.

Now, Japan's reputation for long-sighted, socially controlled investment always exaggerated the reality. Real estate speculators, often getting an extra edge by paying off politicians, and another extra edge through *yakuza* connections, have been a surprisingly important part of the Japanese scene for as long as anyone can remember. Speculative investments in real estate came close to provoking a banking crisis in the 1970s; the situation was saved only through a burst of inflation, which reduced the real value of the speculators' debts and turned bad loans good again. Still, the sheer extent of Japan's bubble was astonishing. Was there some explanation of the phenomenon that ran beyond mere crowd psychology?

Well, it turns out that Japan's bubble was only one of several outbreaks of speculative fever around the world during the 1980s. All of these outbreaks had the common feature that they were financed mainly by bank loans—in particular, that traditionally staid institutions started offering credit to risk-loving, even shady operators in return for somewhat above-market interest rates. The most famous case was that of America's savings and loan associations—institutions whose public image used to be defined by the all-American earnestness of Jimmy Stewart's small-town banker in *It's a Wonderful Life*, but which in the 1980s became identified instead with high-rolling Texas real estate moguls. But similar outbreaks of dubious lending occurred elsewhere, notably in Sweden, another country not usually associated with speculative fever. And economists have long argued that behind all such episodes lies the same economic principle—one, like the basic baby-sitting model of a recession, that will reappear several times in this book. The principle is known as moral hazard.

The term "moral hazard" has its origins in the insurance industry. Very early in the game providers of fire insurance, in particular, noticed that property owners who were fully insured against loss had an interesting tendency to have destructive fires—particularly when changing conditions had reduced the probable market value of their building to less than the insurance coverage. (In the mid-1980s New York City had a number of known "arson-prone" landlords, some of whom would buy a building at an inflated price from a dummy company they themselves owned, use that price as the basis for a large insurance policy, then just happen to have a fire. Moral hazard, indeed.) Eventually the term came to refer to any situation in which one person makes the decision about how much risk to take, while someone else bears the cost if things go badly.

Borrowed money is inherently likely to produce moral hazard. Suppose that I'm a smart guy, but without any capital, and that based on my evident cleverness you decide to lend me a billion dollars, to invest any way I see fit, as long as I promise to repay in a year's time. Even if you charge me a high rate of interest, this is a great deal: I will take the billion, put it into something that *might* make a lot of money, but then again might end up worthless, and hope for the best. If the investment prospers, so will I; if it does not, I will declare personal bankruptcy, and walk away. Heads I win, tails you lose.

Of course, that is why nobody will lend someone without capital of his own a billion dollars to invest as he sees fit, no matter how smart he may seem. Creditors normally place restrictions on what borrowers can do with any money they lend, and borrowers are also normally obliged to put up substantial amounts of their own money, in order to give them a good reason to avoid losses.

Sometimes lenders seem to forget about these rules and lend large sums, no questions asked, to people who put on a good show of knowing what they are doing. We'll get to the amazing story of the hedge funds in Chapter 6. At other times the requirement that the borrower put up enough of his own money can itself be a source of market instability. When assets lose value, those who bought them with borrowed money can be faced with a "margin call": they must either put more of their own money in or repay their creditors by selling the assets, driving the prices down still further, a process that has been central to the current financial crisis. But leaving such market pathologies aside, there is another reason why the rules sometimes get broken: because the moral hazard game is played at taxpayers' expense.

Remember what we said about the main banks of Japanese *keiretsu*: that their depositors believed that their deposits were safe because the government stood behind them. The same is true of almost all banks in the First World, and most banks elsewhere. Modern nations, even if they do not explicitly guarantee deposits, cannot find it in their hearts to let widows and orphans lose their life savings simply because they put them in the wrong bank, just as they cannot bring themselves to stand aside when the raging river sweeps away houses foolishly built in the flood plain. Only the most hard-nosed of conservatives would wish it otherwise. But the result is that people are careless about where they build their houses, and even more careless about where they store their money.

This carelessness offers a tempting opportunity to unscrupulous businessmen: just open a bank, making sure that it has an impressive building and a fancy name. Attract a lot of deposits, by paying good interest if that is allowed, by offering toasters or whatever if it isn't. Then lend the money out, at high interest rates, to high-rolling speculators (preferably friends of yours, or maybe even yourself behind a different corporate front). The depositors won't ask about the quality of your investments since they know that they are protected in any case. And you now have a one-way option: if the investments do well, you become rich; if they do badly, you can simply walk away and let the government clean up the mess.

Okay, it's not that easy, because government regulators aren't entirely stupid. In fact, from the 1930s to the 1980s this kind of behavior was quite rare among bankers because regulators did more or less the same things that a private lender would normally do before handing me a billion dollars to play with. They restricted what banks could do with depositors' money in an effort to prevent excessive risk-taking. They required that the owners of banks put substantial amounts of their own money at stake, through capital requirements. And in a more subtle, perhaps unintentional measure, regulators historically limited the amount of competition among banks, making a banking license a valuable thing in itself, possessed of a considerable "franchise value"; licensees were loath to jeopardize this franchise value by taking risks that could break the bank.

But in the 1980s these restraints broke down in many places. Mainly the cause was deregulation. Traditional banks were safe, but also very conservative; arguably they failed to direct capital to its most productive uses. The cure, argued reformers, was both more freedom and more competition: let banks lend where they thought best, and allow more players to compete for public savings. Somehow reformers forgot that this would give banks more freedom to take bad risks and that by reducing their franchise value it would give them less incentive to avoid them. Changes in the marketplace, notably the rise of alternative sources of corporate finance, further eroded the profit margins of bankers who clung to safe, old-fashioned ways of doing businesses.

And so in the 1980s there was a sort of global epidemic of moral hazard. Few countries can be proud of their handling of the situation—surely not the United States, whose mishandling of the savings and loan affair was a classic case of imprudent, shortsighted, and occasionally corrupt policymaking. But Japan, where all the usual lines—between government and business, between

banks and their clients, between what was and what was not subject to government guarantee—were especially blurry, was peculiarly ill suited to a loosened financial regime. Japan's banks lent
more, with less regard for quality of the borrower, than anyone
else's. In so doing they helped inflate the bubble economy to gro-
tesque proportions.

Sooner or later, bubbles always burst. The bursting of the Japanese bubble wasn't entirely spontaneous: the Bank of Japan, concerned about speculative excess, began raising interest rates in
1990 in an effort to let some of the air out of the balloon. At first
this policy was unsuccessful, but beginning in 1991 land and stock
prices began a steep decline, which within a few years brought
them some 60 percent below their peak.

Initially, and indeed for several years thereafter, Japanese authorities seem to have regarded all of this as healthy—a return to more
sensible, realistic asset valuations. But it gradually became apparent that the end of the bubble economy had brought not economic
health but a steadily deepening malaise.

A Stealthy Depression

Unlike Mexico in 1995, South Korea in 1998, and Argentina in
2002, Japan never went through a year of unmistakable, catastrophic economic decline. In the decade after the bubble burst,
Japan experienced only two years in which real GDP actually fell.

But year after year growth fell short, not just of the economy's
previous experience but of any reasonable estimate of the growth
in its capacity. There was one year in the decade after 1991 in
which Japan grew as fast as it did in an *average* year in the preceding decade. Even if you take a conservative estimate of the growth
in Japan's "potential output," the output the economy could have

produced with full employment of resources, there was also only one year in which actual output grew as rapidly as potential.

Economists have one of their famously awkward phrases for what Japan was experiencing: a "growth recession." A growth recession is what happens when an economy grows but this growth isn't fast enough to keep up with the economy's expanding capacity, so that more and more machines and workers stand idle. Normally growth recessions are rather rare, because both booms and slumps tend to gather momentum, producing either rapid growth or clear-cut decline. Japan, however, essentially experienced a decade-long growth recession, which left it so far below where it should have been that it verged on a new phenomenon: a growth depression.

The slowness with which Japan's economy deteriorated was in itself a source of much confusion. Because the depression crept up on the country, there was never a moment at which the public clamored for the government to do something dramatic. Because Japan's economic engine gradually lost power rather than coming to a screeching halt, the government itself consistently defined success down, regarding the economy's continuing growth as a vindication of its policies even though that growth was well short of what could and should have been achieved. And at the same time, both Japanese and foreign analysts tended to assume that because the economy grew so slowly for so long, it *couldn't* grow any faster.

So Japan's economic policies were marked by an odd combination of smugness and fatalism—and by a noticeable unwillingness to think hard about how things could have gone so very wrong.

Japan's Trap

There is nothing mysterious about the onset of Japan's slump in 1991: sooner or later the financial bubble was bound to burst, and when it did it would bring about a decline in investment, in consumption, and hence in overall demand. The same thing happened in the United States after the U.S. stock market bubble of the 1990s burst, and again after the next decade's housing bubble popped. The question, however, is why Japan's policymakers, in particular its central bank, weren't able to get the economy moving again.

It is time to return to the story of the baby-sitting co-op. Suppose that the U.S. stock market were to crash, undermining consumer confidence. Would this inevitably mean a disastrous recession? Think of it this way: when consumer confidence declines, it is as if for some reason the typical member of the co-op had become less willing to go out, more anxious to accumulate coupons for a rainy day. This could indeed lead to a slump—but need not, if the management were alert and responded by simply issuing more coupons. That is exactly what our head coupon issuer, Alan Greenspan, did in 1987.

Or suppose that the coupon issuer didn't respond quickly enough, and that the economy did indeed fall into a slump. Don't panic: even if the head coupon issuer temporarily gets behind the curve, he can still ordinarily turn the situation around by issuing more coupons— that is, with a vigorous monetary expansion, like the ones that ended the U.S. recessions of 1981–82, 1990–91, and 2001.

What about all the bad investments made during the boom? Well, that was so much wasted capital. But there is no obvious reason why bad investments made in the past require an actual slump in output in the present. Productive capacity may not have risen as much as anticipated, but it has not actually fallen; why not just print enough money to keep spending up so that the economy makes full use of the capacity it has?

Remember, the story of the co-op tells you that economic

slumps are not punishments for our sins, pains that we are fated to suffer. The Capitol Hill co-op didn't get into trouble because its members were bad, inefficient baby-sitters; its troubles did not reveal the fundamental flaws of "Capitol Hill values" or "crony baby-sittingism." It had a technical problem—too many people chasing too little scrip—which could be, and was, solved with a little clear thinking. And so the co-op's story ought to inoculate us against fatalism and pessimism. It seems to imply that recessions are always, and indeed easily, curable.

But in that case why didn't Japan pull up its socks after the bubble burst? How could Japan get stuck in a seemingly intractable slump—one that it didn't appear able to get out of simply by printing coupons? Well, if we extend the co-op's story a little bit, it is not hard to generate something that looks a lot like Japan's problems.

First, we have to imagine a co-op whose members realized that there was an unnecessary inconvenience in their system: there would be occasions when a couple would find itself needing to go out several times in a row, and would run out of coupons—and therefore would be unable to get its babies sat—even though it was entirely willing to do lots of compensatory baby-sitting at a later date. To resolve this problem, we'll suppose the co-op allowed members to *borrow* extra coupons from the management in times of need, repaying with the coupons received from subsequent baby-sitting. (We could move the story a bit closer to the way real economies work by imagining that couples could also borrow coupons from each other; the interest rate in this infant capital market would then play the role the "discount rate" of the co-op management plays in our parable.) To prevent members from abusing this privilege, however, the management would need to impose some penalty, requiring borrowers to repay more coupons than they borrowed.

Under this new system, couples would hold smaller reserves of coupons than before, knowing that they could borrow more if necessary. The co-op's officers would, however, have acquired a new tool of management. If members of the co-op reported that it was easy to find baby-sitters, hard to find opportunities to baby-sit, the terms under which members could borrow coupons could be made more favorable, encouraging more people to go out. If baby-sitters were scarce, those terms could be worsened, encouraging people to go out less.

In other words, this more sophisticated co-op would have a central bank that could stimulate a depressed economy by reducing the interest rate, cool off an overheated one by raising it.

But in Japan interest rates fell almost to zero, and still the economy slumped. Have we finally exhausted the usefulness of our parable?

Well, imagine that there is a seasonality in the demand and supply for baby-sitting. During the winter, when it's cold and dark, couples don't want to go out much but are quite willing to stay home and look after other people's children—thereby accumulating points they can use on balmy summer evenings. If this seasonality isn't too pronounced, the co-op could still keep the supply and demand for baby-sitting in balance by charging low interest rates in the winter months, higher rates in the summer. But suppose that the seasonality is very strong indeed. Then in the winter, even at a zero interest rate, there will be more couples seeking opportunities to baby-sit than there are couples going out, which means that baby-sitting opportunities will be hard to find, which means that couples seeking to build up reserves for summer fun will be even less willing to use those points in the winter, meaning even fewer opportunities to baby-sit . . . and the co-op will slide into a recession even at a zero interest rate.

And the 1990s were the winter of Japan's discontent. Perhaps because of its aging population, perhaps also because of a general nervousness about the future, the Japanese public didn't appear willing to spend enough to use the economy's capacity, even at a zero interest rate. Japan, say the economists, fell into the dread "liquidity trap." And what you have just read is an infantile explanation of what a liquidity trap is and how it can happen.

Japan Adrift

The standard response to a recession is to cut interest rates—to allow people to borrow baby-sitting coupons cheaply so that they will begin going out again. Japan was slow to cut interest rates after the bubble burst, but it eventually cut them all the way to zero, and it still wasn't enough. Now what?

The classic answer, the one that has been associated with the name of John Maynard Keynes, is that if the private sector won't spend enough to maintain full employment, the public sector must take up the slack. Let the government borrow money and use the funds to finance public investment projects—if possible to good purpose, but that is a secondary consideration—and thereby provide jobs, which will make people more willing to spend, which will generate still more jobs, and so on. The Great Depression in the United States was brought to an end by a massive deficit-financed public works program, known as World War II. Why not try to jump-start Japanese growth with a more pacific version of the same?

Japan tried. During the 1990s the government produced a series of stimulus packages, borrowing money to build roads and bridges whether the country needed them or not. These packages created jobs directly and boosted the economy as a whole every time they were tried.

The trouble was that the programs didn't get enough bang for the yen. In 1991 Japan's government was running a fairly hefty budget surplus (2.9 percent of GDP). By 1996 it was running a quite nasty deficit of 4.3 percent of GDP. Yet the economic engine was still sputtering. Meanwhile, the ever-growing deficits were starting to worry Japan's Ministry of Finance, which was concerned about the long-term budget position. The big concern was demographics (which may also have a lot to do with Japan's high savings and low investment demand). Like other countries, Japan had a baby boom followed by a baby bust, and faces the prospect of a rising ratio of retirees to workers. But Japan's problem is extreme: its working-age population is actually declining steadily, even as the number of retirees rapidly grows. And since retired citizens are a heavy fiscal burden on modern governments—recipients of expensive public pensions and health care—standard fiscal principles said that Japan should be building up a trust fund to meet the future bills, not running ever-growing deficits.

In 1997 the voices of fiscal responsibility prevailed, and Prime Minister Ryutaro Hashimoto increased taxes to reduce the budget deficit. The economy promptly plunged into recession.

So it was back to deficit spending. In 1998 Japan introduced a massive new program of public works. But the fiscal issue had now been raised, and it refused to go away. Investors soon noticed that Japan was projecting a deficit of 10 percent of GDP, and that the ratio of government debt to GDP was already above 100 percent. These are the kinds of numbers usually associated with Latin American nations at risk of hyperinflation. Nobody really expected hyperinflation in Japan, but investors were getting at least a bit worried about the long-term soundness of that government's finances. In short, the attempt to jump-start the economy with deficit spending seemed to be reaching its limits.

What other options were there?

If government spending is one standard response to a stalled economy, pumping up the banks is another. One widely held view about the Great Depression is that it persisted so long because the banking crises of 1930–31 inflicted long-term damage to credit markets. According to this view, there were businessmen who would have been willing to spend more if they could have gotten access to credit, and who would in fact have been qualified borrowers. But the bankers who could have made those loans were themselves either out of business or unable to raise funds because the public's confidence in banks had been so shaken. In terms of the baby-sitting co-op, this amounts to saying that there were people who would have been willing to go out in the winter and baby-sit in the summer, but who could not get anybody to lend them the necessary coupons.

Now, Japan's banks made a lot of bad loans in the bubble economy years, and the long stagnation that followed turned many other loans bad as well. So one theory of Japan's slump was that the country was in a liquidity trap mainly because its banks were financially weak; fix the banks and the economy would recover. And in late 1998 Japan's legislature put together a $500 billion bank rescue plan.

Yet another option for Japan was to do whatever it took to get a bit of inflation going. This option needs some explaining.

The truth is that economists didn't think much about the subject of liquidity traps for a very long time. Before Japan's troubles in the 1990s, the last time a major economy appeared to be in such a trap was the United States in the late 1930s. And economic historians have tended to downplay the significance of that experience by arguing either that it wasn't a true liquidity trap—that the Fed could have gotten us out if it had tried hard enough—or that we got into that trap only through extraordinary policy mistakes, unlikely to be repeated. So as the outlines of Japan's trap became clear in the mid-1990s, economists were basically unprepared— and, if I may be critical of my profession, uninterested. I continue to be astonished at how few economists around the world realized just how important a problem Japan's trap was both as a practical matter and as a challenge to our economic doctrines.

But economics is, as the great Victorian economist Alfred Marshall said, "not a body of concrete truth, but an engine for the discovery of concrete truth." Or to put it in less elevated language, old models can be taught to perform new tricks. As we saw in my revised version of the baby-sitting story, a model designed to explain why a central bank can normally cure a recession by cutting interest rates can also illuminate the circumstances under which this over-the-counter remedy does not work. And this revised parable also, it turns out, offers some guidance on ways to get out of a liquidity trap, or at least on how to avoid getting into one in the first place .

Remember, the basic problem with the baby-sitting co-op is that people want to save the credit they earn from baby-sitting in the winter to use in the summer, even at a zero interest rate. But in the aggregate the co-op's members *can't* save up winter baby-sitting for summer use; so individual efforts to do so end up producing nothing but a winter slump.

The answer, as any economist should immediately realize, is to get the price right: to make it clear that points earned in the winter will be devalued if held until the summer—say, to make five hours of baby-sitting credit earned in the winter melt into only four hours by summer. This will encourage people to use their baby-sitting hours sooner, and hence create more baby-sitting opportunities. You might be tempted to think that there is something unfair about this—that it means expropriating people's savings. But the reality is that the co-op as a whole *cannot* bank winter baby-sitting for summer use, so it is actually distorting members' incentives to allow them to trade winter for summer hours on a one-for-one basis.

But what in the non-baby-sitting economy corresponds to our coupons that melt in the summer? The answer is *inflation*, which causes the real value of money to melt away over time. Or to be more precise, one thing that can get an economy out of a liquidity trap is *expected* inflation, which discourages people from hoarding money. Once you take the possibility of a liquidity trap seriously— and the case of Japan makes it clear that we should—it's impossible to escape the conclusion that expected inflation can be a good thing, because it helps you get out of the trap. I have explained the virtues of inflation in terms of the whimsical parable of the baby-sitting co-op, but the same conclusion also pops out from application of any of the standard mathematical models that economists conventionally use to discuss monetary policy. Indeed, there has long been a strand of thought that says that moderate inflation may be necessary if monetary policy is to be able to fight recessions. Still, advocates of inflation have had to contend with a deep-seated sense that stable prices are always desirable, that to promote inflation is to create perverse and dangerous incentives. This belief in the importance of price stability is not based on standard economic models—on the contrary, the usual textbook theory, when applied to Japan's unusual circumstances, points directly to inflation as the natural solution. But conventional economic theory and conventional economic wisdom are not always the same thing—a conflict that would become increasingly apparent as one country after another found itself having to make hard choices in the face of financial crisis.

Japan's Recovery

Japan's economy finally began to show some signs of recovery around 2003. Real GDP started growing at slightly more than 2 percent a year, unemployment came down, and the grinding deflation afflicting the economy (and worsening the liquidity trap) abated, although there was no sign of actual inflation. What went right?

The answer, mainly, was exports. In the middle years of this decade the United States ran huge trade deficits, importing vast quantities of manufactured goods. Some of these goods came from Japan, although the biggest growth came in imports from China and other emerging economies. But Japan benefited from Chinese growth too, because many Chinese manufactured goods contain components made in Japan. One flip side of America's import boom, then, was rising Japanese exports and a recovering Japanese economy.

Japan's escape from its trap remained provisional, however. The call money rate in Japan, the equivalent of the Federal funds rate (the rate set by the Federal Reserve), was only 0.5 percent at the time of writing. This meant that the Bank of Japan had very little room to cut interest rates in the face of the recession that seemed to be looming. And if the recession is deep, Japan will be right back in its trap.

4

ASIA'S CRASH

Thailand isn't really a small country. It has more citizens than Britain or France; Bangkok is a vast urban nightmare whose traffic is every bit as bad as legend has it. Still, the world economy is almost inconceivably huge, and in the commercial scheme of things Thailand is pretty marginal. Despite rapid growth in the 1980s and 1990s, it is still a poor country; all those people have a combined purchasing power no greater than that of the population of Massachusetts. One might have thought that Thai economic affairs, unlike those of an economic behemoth like Japan, were of interest only to the Thais, their immediate neighbors, and those businesses with a direct financial stake in the country.

But the 1997 devaluation of Thailand's currency, the baht, triggered a financial avalanche that buried much of Asia. The crucial questions are why that happened and, indeed, how it even *could* have happened. But before we get to why and how, let's review what: the story of Thailand's boom, its crash, and the spread of that crash across Asia.

The Boom

Thailand was a relative latecomer to the Asian miracle. Traditionally mainly an agricultural exporter, it started to become a major industrial center only in the 1980s, when foreign firms—especially Japanese—began siting plants in the country. But when the economy did take off, it did so very impressively: as peasants moved from the countryside into the new urban jobs, as the good results experienced by the first wave of foreign investors encouraged others to follow, Thailand began growing at 8 percent or more per year. Soon the famed temples of Bangkok lay in the shadow of office and apartment towers. Like its neighbors, Thailand became a place where millions of ordinary people were beginning to emerge from desperate poverty into at least the beginnings of a decent life, and where some people were becoming very rich.

Until the early 1990s, most of the investment associated with this growth came from the savings of the Thais themselves. Foreign money built the big export factories, but the smaller businesses were financed by local businessmen out of their own savings, and the new office and apartment blocks were financed out of the bank deposits of domestic households. In 1991 Thailand's foreign debt was slightly less than its annual exports—not a trivial ratio but one that was well within normal bounds of safety. (In the same year Latin American debt averaged 2.7 times exports.)

During the 1990s, however, Thailand's financial self-sufficiency began to erode. The push mainly came from outside. The resolution of the Latin debt crisis, described in Chapter 2, made investment in the Third World respectable again. The fall of Communism, by

diminishing the perceived threat of radical takeover, made investing outside the safety of the Western world seem less risky than
before. In the early 1990s interest rates in advanced countries were
exceptionally low because central banks were trying to boot their
economies out of a mild recession, and many investors went abroad
in search of higher yields. Perhaps most crucial of all, investment
funds coined a new name for what had previously been called Third
World or developing countries: now they were "emerging markets,"
the new frontier of financial opportunity.

Investors responded in droves. In 1990 private capital flows to
developing countries were $42 billion, and official agencies like the
International Monetary Fund and the World Bank financed more
investment in the Third World than all private investors combined.
By 1997, however, while the flow of official money had actually
slowed, the flow of private capital to developing countries had
quintupled, to $256 billion. At first most of the money went to
Latin America, especially Mexico, but after 1994 it increasingly
went to the apparently safer economies of Southeast Asia.

How did the money get from Tokyo or Frankfurt to Bangkok or
Djakarta? (Most of the lending to Asia was Japanese or European
—through wisdom or luck, U.S. banks mainly stayed on the sidelines.) What did it do when it got there? Let's follow the steps.

Start with a typical transaction: A Japanese bank makes a loan
to a Thai "finance company," an institution whose main purpose is
to act as a conveyor belt for foreign funds. The finance company
now has yen, which it uses to make a loan at a higher interest rate,
to a local real estate developer. But the developer wants to borrow
baht, not yen, since he must buy land and pay his workers in local
currency. So the finance company goes to the foreign exchange
market and exchanges its yen for baht.

Now, the foreign exchange market, like other markets, is governed by the law of supply and demand: increase the demand for something, and its price will normally rise. That is, the demand for baht by the finance company will tend to make the baht rise in value against other currencies. But during the boom years Thailand's central bank was committed to maintaining a stable rate of exchange between the baht and the U.S. dollar. To do this, it would have to offset any increase in the demand for baht by also increasing the supply: selling baht and buying foreign currencies like the dollar or yen. So the indirect result of that initial yen loan would be an increase both in the Bank of Thailand's reserves of foreign exchange and in the Thai money supply. And there would also be an expansion of credit in the economy—not only the loan directly provided by the finance company but also additional credit provided by the banks in which the newly created baht were deposited. And since much of the money lent out would itself end up back in the banks in the form of new deposits, this would finance yet further new loans, and so on, in the classic "money multiplier" process taught in Econ 101. (My description of Argentina's 1995 banking crisis was an example of this same process running in reverse.)

As more and more loans poured in from abroad, then, the result was a massive expansion of credit, which fueled a wave of new investment. Some of this took the form of actual construction, mainly office and apartment buildings, but there was a lot of pure speculation too, mainly in real estate, but also in stocks. By early 1996 the economies of Southeast Asia were starting to bear a strong family resemblance to Japan's "bubble economy" of the late 1980s.

Why didn't the monetary authorities put curbs on the speculative boom? The answer is that they tried but failed. In all the Asian economies, central banks tried to "sterilize" the capital inflows: obliged to sell baht in the foreign exchange market, the Bank of

Thailand would try to buy those baht back elsewhere by selling bonds, in effect borrowing back the money it had just printed. But this borrowing drove up local interest rates, making borrowing from overseas even more attractive and pulling in yet more yen and dollars. The effort to sterilize failed: credit just kept on growing.

The only way the central bank could have prevented money and credit from ballooning would have been to stop trying to fix the exchange rate—to simply let the baht rise. And this is indeed what many Monday-morning quarterbacks now say the Thais should have done. But at the time this seemed like a bad idea: a stronger baht would make Thai exports less competitive on world markets (because wages and other costs would be higher in dollars), and in general the Thais thought that a stable exchange rate was good for business confidence, that they were too small a nation to endure the kind of widely fluctuating exchange rate the United States lives with.

And so the boom was allowed to run its course. Eventually, as an economics textbook would tell you, the expansion of money and credit was self-limiting. Soaring investment, together with a surge of spending by newly affluent consumers, led to a surge in imports, while the booming economy pulled up wages, making Thai exports less competitive (especially because China, an important competitor for Thailand, had devalued its own currency in 1994). So export growth slowed down. The result was a huge trade deficit. Instead of feeding domestic money and credit, those foreign-currency loans started paying for imports.

And why not? Some economists argued—just as Mexico's boosters had argued in the early 1990s—that the trade deficits of Thailand, Malaysia, and Indonesia were a sign not of economic weakness but of economic strength, of markets working the way they were supposed to. To repeat the argument: as a matter of sheer accounting, a country that is attracting net inflows of capital must be running a current account deficit of equal size. So as long as you thought that the capital inflows to Southeast Asia were economically justified, so were the trade deficits. And why wasn't it reasonable for the world to invest a lot of capital in Southeast Asia, given the region's record of growth and economic stability? After all, this wasn't a case of governments on a spending spree: while Malaysia and Indonesia had their share of grandiose public projects, they were being paid for out of current revenue, and budgets were more or less in balance. So these trade deficits were the product of private-sector decisions; why should these decisions be second-guessed?

Still, a growing number of observers started to feel a bit uneasy as the deficits of Thailand and Malaysia grew to 6, 7, 8 percent of GDP—the sorts of numbers Mexico had had before the tequila crisis. The Mexican experience had convinced some economists that international capital flows, even if they represented the undistorted decisions of the private sector, were not necessarily to be trusted. The bullishness of investors about Asian prospects bore a disturbing resemblance to their bullishness about Latin America a couple of years earlier. And the Mexican experience also suggested that a reversal of market sentiment, when it came, would be sharp and hard to deal with.

What we also should have noticed was that the claim that Asian borrowing represented free private-sector decisions was not quite the truth. For Southeast Asia, like Japan in the bubble years, had a moral hazard problem—the problem that would soon be dubbed crony capitalism.

Let's go back to that Thai finance company, the institution that borrowed the yen that started the whole process of credit expansion. What, exactly, were these finance companies? They were not, as it happens, ordinary banks: by and large they had few if any depositors. Nor were they like Western investment banks, repositories of specialized information that could help direct funds to their most profitable uses. So what was their reason for existence? What did they bring to the table?

The answer, basically, was political connections—often, indeed, the owner of the finance company was a relative of some government official. And so the claim that the decisions about how much to borrow and invest represented private-sector judgments, not to be second-guessed, rang more than a bit hollow. True, loans to finance companies were not subject to the kind of formal guarantees that backed deposits in U.S. savings and loans. But foreign banks that lent money to the minister's nephew's finance company can be forgiven for believing that they had a little extra protection, that the minister would find a way to rescue the company if its investments did not work out as planned. And the foreign lenders would have been right: in roughly nine out of ten cases, foreign lenders to finance companies did indeed get bailed out by the Thai government when the crisis came.

Now look at the situation from the point of view of the minister's nephew, the owner of the finance company. Basically, he was in a position to borrow money at low rates, no questions asked. What, then, could be more natural than to lend that money at a high rate of interest to his friend the real estate developer, whose speculative new office tower just might make a killing—but then again might not. If all went well, fine: both men would have made a lot of money. If things did not turn out as hoped, well, not so terrible: the minister would find a way to save the finance company. Heads the nephew wins, tails the taxpayer loses.

One way or another, similar games were being played in all the countries that would soon be caught up in the crisis. In Indonesia middlemen played less of a role: there the typical dubious transaction was a direct loan from a foreign bank to a company controlled by one of the president's cronies. (The quintessential example was the loan that broke Hong Kong's Peregrine Investment Holdings, a loan made directly to Suharto's daughter's taxi company.) In Korea the big borrowers were banks effectively controlled by *chaebol*, the huge conglomerates that have dominated the nation's economy and—until very recently—its politics. Throughout the region, then, implicit government guarantees were helping underwrite investments that were both riskier and less promising than would have been undertaken without those guarantees, adding fuel to what would probably anyway have been an overheated speculative boom.

Given all of this, the development of some kind of crisis was not too surprising. Some of us can even claim to have predicted currency crises more than a year in advance. But nobody realized just how severe the crisis would be.

July 2, 1997

During 1996 and the first half of 1997 the credit machine that had created Thailand's boom began to slip into reverse. Partly this was because of external events: markets for some of Thailand's exports went soft, a depreciation of Japan's yen made Southeast Asian industry a bit less competitive. Mostly, though, it was simply a matter of the house beating the gamblers, which in the long run it always does: a growing number of the speculative investments that had been financed, directly or indirectly, by cheap foreign loans went sour. Some speculators went bust, and some finance companies went out of business. Foreign lenders became increasingly reluctant to lend any more money.

The loss of confidence was to a certain extent a self-reinforcing process. As long as real estate prices and stock markets were booming, even questionable investments tended to look good. As the air began to go out of the bubble, losses began to mount, further reducing confidence and causing the supply of fresh loans to shrink even more. Even before the July 2 crisis, land and stock values had fallen a long way from their peaks.

The slowdown in foreign borrowing also posed problems for the central bank. With fewer yen and dollars coming in, the demand for baht on the foreign exchange market declined; meanwhile, the need to change baht into foreign currencies to pay for imports continued unabated. In order to keep the value of the baht from declining, the Bank of Thailand had to do the opposite of what it had done when capital starting coming in: it went into the market to exchange dollars and yen for baht, supporting its own currency. But there is an important difference between trying to keep your currency down and trying to keep it up: the Bank of Thailand can increase the supply of baht as much as it likes, because it can simply print them; but it cannot print dollars. So there was a limit on its ability to keep the baht up. Sooner or later it would run out of reserves.

The only way to sustain the value of the currency would have been to reduce the number of baht in circulation, driving up interest rates and thus making it attractive once again to borrow dollars to reinvest in baht. But this posed problems of a different sort. As the investment boom sputtered out, the Thai economy had slowed—there was less construction activity, which meant fewer jobs, which meant lower income, which meant layoffs in the rest of the economy. Although it wasn't quite a full-fledged recession, the economy was no longer living in the style to which it had become accustomed. To raise interest rates would be to discourage investment further, and perhaps push the economy into an unambiguous slump.

The alternative was to let the currency go: to stop buying baht and let the exchange rate slide. But this too was an unattractive option, not only because a devaluation of the currency would hurt the government's reputation but also because so many banks, finance companies, and other Thai businesses had debts in dollars. If the value of the dollar in terms of baht were to increase, many of them would find themselves insolvent.

So the Thai government dithered. It wasn't willing to let the baht fall; nor was it willing to take the kind of harsh domestic measures that would have stemmed the loss in reserves. Instead, it played a waiting game, apparently hoping that something would eventually turn up.

All of this was according to the standard script: it was the classic lead-in to a currency crisis, of the kind that economists love to model—and speculators love to provoke. As it became clear that the government did not have the stomach to turn the screws on the domestic economy, it became increasingly likely that eventually the baht would be allowed to fall in value. But since it hadn't happened yet, there was still time to take advantage of the prospective event. As long as the baht-dollar exchange rate seemed likely to remain stable, the fact that interest rates in Thailand were several points higher than in the United States provided an incentive to borrow in dollars and lend in baht. But once it became a high probability that the baht would soon be devalued, the incentive was to go the other way—to borrow in baht, expecting that the dollar value of these debts would soon be reduced, and acquire dollars, expecting that the baht value of these assets would soon increase. Local businessmen borrowed in baht and paid off their dollar loans; wealthy Thais sold their holdings of government debt and bought U.S. Treasury bills; and last but not least, some large international hedge funds began borrowing baht and converting the proceeds into dollars.

All of these actions involved selling baht and buying other currencies, which meant that they required the central bank to buy even more baht to keep the currency from falling, which depleted its reserves of foreign exchange even faster—which further reinforced the conviction that the baht was going to be devalued sooner rather than later. A classic currency crisis was in full swing.

Any money doctor can tell you that once things have reached that point the government must move decisively, one way or the other: either make a clear commitment to defend the currency at all costs, or let it go. But governments usually have a hard time making either decision. Like many governments before and no doubt many to come, Thailand's waited as its reserves ran down; trying to convince markets that its position was stronger than it was, it made those reserves look larger through unannounced "currency swaps" (in effect, borrowing dollars now for repayment later). But though the pressure sometimes seemed to abate, it always resumed. By the beginning of July, it was clear that the game was up. On July 2, the Thais let the baht go.

Up to this point, nothing all that surprising had happened. The rundown of reserves, the speculative attack on an obviously weak currency, were right out of the textbooks. But despite the recent experience of the tequila crisis, most people thought that the devaluation of the baht would pretty much end the story: a humiliation for the government, perhaps a nasty shock for some overstretched businesses, but nothing catastrophic. Surely Thailand looked nothing like Mexico. Nobody could accuse it of having achieved "stabilization, reform, and no growth"; there was no Thai Cárdenas, waiting in the wings to enforce a populist program. And so there would not be a devastating recession.

They were wrong.

Meltdown

There are two somewhat different questions to ask about the recession that spread across Asia in the wake of the Thai devaluation. The first is one of mechanics: How did this slump happen? Why should a devaluation in one small economy have provoked a collapse of investment and output across so wide an area? The other, in a way deeper, question is, Why didn't governments, or perhaps why couldn't governments, prevent the catastrophe? What happened to macroeconomic policy?

That second question will take some time to answer, at least partly because it is a matter of very sharp disagreement among reasonable people. So let's leave it until the next chapter, and simply try to describe what happened.

When all goes well, nothing terrible happens when a currency is allowed to drop in value. When Britain abandoned its defense of the pound in 1992, the currency dropped about 15 percent, then stabilized: investors figured that the worst was over, that the lower currency would help the country's exports, and that it was therefore a better place to invest than it had been before. Typical calculations suggested that the baht would have to fall something like 15 percent to make Thai industry cost-competitive again, so a decline of roughly that magnitude seemed likely. But instead, the currency went into free fall: the baht price of a dollar soared 50 percent over the next few months, and would have risen even further if Thailand had not sharply raised interest rates.

Why did the baht fall so far? The short answer is "panic"; but there are panics and there are panics. Which was it?

Sometimes a panic is just a panic: an irrational reaction on the part of investors that is not justified by the actual news. An example might be the brief plunge in the dollar in 1981, after a deranged gunman wounded Ronald Reagan. It was a shocking event; but even if Reagan had died, the stability of the U.S. government and the continuity of its policy could hardly have been affected. Those who kept their heads and did not flee the dollar were rewarded for their cool heads.

Much more important in economics, however, are panics that, whatever sets them off, validate themselves—because the panic itself makes panic justified. The classic example is a bank run: when all of a bank's depositors try to withdraw their money at once, the bank is forced to sell its assets at distress prices, causing it to go bankrupt; those depositors who did not panic end up worse off than those who did.

And indeed there *were* some bank runs in Thailand, and even more in Indonesia. But to focus only on these bank runs would be to take the metaphor too literally. What really happened was a circular process—a devastating feedback loop—of financial deterioration and declining confidence, of which conventional bank runs were only one aspect.

The figure on the next page illustrates this process, which occurred in some version in all of the afflicted Asian economies, schematically. Start anywhere in the circle—say, with a decline of confidence in Thailand's currency and economy. This decline in confidence would make investors, both domestic and foreign, want to pull their money out of the country. Other things being the same, this would cause the baht to plunge in value. Since the Thai

The Vicious Circle of Financial Crisis

central bank could no longer support the value of its currency by buying it on the foreign exchange market (because it no longer had dollars or yen to spend), the only way it could limit the currency's decline was to raise interest rates and pull baht out of circulation. Unfortunately, both the decline in the currency's value and the rise in interest rates created financial problems for businesses, both financial institutions and other companies. On one side, many of them had dollar debts, which suddenly became more burdensome as the number of baht per dollar increased; on the other, many of them also had baht debts, which became harder to service as interest rates soared. And the combination of higher interest rates and troubled balance sheets with a banking system that often found itself unable to make even the safest of loans meant that companies had to slash spending, causing a recession, which in turn meant still worse news for profits and balance sheets. All this bad news from the economy, inevitably, reduced confidence still further—and the economy went into a meltdown.

Leaving aside all the complicated details (which are still being picked over by researchers), this story seems fairly straightforward —especially because something quite similar happened in Mexico in 1995. So why did the disastrous effects of Thailand's devaluation come as such a surprise? The basic answer is that while many economists were aware of the elements of this story—everyone understood that the feedback from confidence, to financial markets, to the real economy, and back again to confidence existed in principle—nobody realized just how powerful that feedback process would be in practice. And as a result nobody realized how explosive the circular logic of crisis could be.

Here's a parallel. A microphone in an auditorium always generates a feedback loop: sounds picked up by the microphone are amplified by the loudspeakers; the output from the speakers is itself picked up by the microphone; and so on. But as long as the room isn't too echoey and the gain isn't too high, this is a "damped" process and poses no problem. Turn the dial a little too far to the right, however, and the process becomes explosive: any little sound is picked up, amplified, picked up again, and suddenly there is an earsplitting screech. What matters, in other words, is not just the qualitative fact of feedback, but its quantitative strength. What caught everyone by surprise was the discovery that the dial was in fact turned up so high.

Indeed, even now there are many people who find it hard to believe that a market economy can really be that unstable, that the feedbacks illustrated in the figure can really be strong enough to create an explosive crisis. But they are—as we can see by looking at the way the crisis spread.

Contagion

There is probably a good reason why important meetings about international finance, especially about international crisis management, tend to take place in rustic resorts—why the postwar monetary system was hammered out at the Mount Washington Hotel at Bretton Woods, why many of the world's finance ministers and central bankers gather each summer at Jackson Lake Lodge in Wyoming. Perhaps the setting helps important people get away from the firefighting of their daily lives and focus at least briefly on the larger issues. In any case, in early October 1997—when the Asian crisis was well underway, but its severity was not yet clear—a number of bankers, officials, and economists converged on Woodstock, Vermont, to take stock.

By then Thailand was already pretty clearly in deep trouble, the currency of its neighbor Malaysia had also been battered, and the Indonesian rupiah had depreciated about 30 percent. The general sense in the room was that Thailand had brought its woes on itself; and there was little sympathy for Malaysia, which like Thailand had been running huge current account deficits in the past several years, and whose prime minister had clearly made things worse with his denunciations of evil speculators. But everyone agreed that while Indonesia had been right to let its currency slide—indeed, many good things were said about Indonesia's economic management— the rupiah's weakness was not really justified. After all, Indonesia's current account deficits had been nowhere near as large relative to GDP as its neighbors'—at less than 4 percent of GDP, Indonesia's 1996 deficit was actually smaller than, say, Australia's. The country's export base—part raw materials, part labor-intensive manufacturing—looked solid; and in general the economy looked fundamentally sound.

Within three months Indonesia was in even worse shape than the rest of Southeast Asia, indeed on its way to one of the worst economic slumps in world history. And the crisis had spread not just across Southeast Asia but all the way to South Korea, a far-away economy whose GDP was twice as large as that of Indonesia, three times as large as that of Thailand.

There are sometimes good reasons for economic contagion. An old line says that when the United States sneezes, Canada catches cold—no wonder, when much of Canada's production is sold in the markets of its giant southern neighbor. And there were some direct links among the afflicted Asian economies: Thailand is a market for Malaysian products and vice versa. A bit of extra traction may have been generated by the tendency of the Asian economies to sell similar products to third parties: when Thailand devalued its currency, the clothing it exports to the West got cheaper, and therefore cut into the profit margins of Indonesian producers of similar items.

But all estimates of this direct, "goods market" spillover among the crisis economies indicate that it just can't have been a major factor in the spread of the crisis. In particular, Thailand's role either as a market for or as a competitor of South Korea was little more than rounding error for the far larger Korean economy.

A more potent source of contagion may have been more or less direct financial linkage. Not that Thais were big investors in Korea, or Koreans in Thailand; but the flows of money into the region were often channeled through "emerging market funds" that lumped all the countries together. When bad news came in from Thailand, money flowed out of these funds, and hence out of all the countries in the region.

Even more important than this mechanical linkage, however, was the way that Asian economies were associated in the minds of investors. The appetite of investors for the region had been fed by the perception of a shared "Asian miracle." When one country's economy turned out not to be all that miraculous after all, it shook faith in all the others. The wise men at Woodstock may have regarded Indonesia as quite different from Thailand, but the investor in the street was less sure and began to pull back just in case.

And it turned out that whatever the differences among all those economies, one thing they did have in common was susceptibility to self-validating panic. The wise men at Woodstock were wrong about Indonesia, and the panicky investors right; this was not because the wise men had misjudged Indonesia's virtues but because they had underestimated its vulnerability. In Malaysia, in Indonesia, in Korea, as in Thailand, the market's loss of confidence started a vicious circle of financial and economic collapse. It did not matter that these economies were only modestly linked in terms of physical flows of goods. They were linked in the minds of investors, who regarded the troubles of one Asian economy as bad news about the others; and when an economy is vulnerable to self-validating panic, believing makes it so.

Why Asia? Why 1997?

Why did Asia experience a terrible economic crisis, and why did it begin in 1997? As Bill Clinton might have put it, the answer depends on what you mean by "why." You might be asking about the specific precipitating events, or you might, more importantly, be asking about the source of Asia's extraordinary vulnerability.

If you insist on placing the blame for the onset of the Asian crisis on some specific event, there is a list of usual suspects. One is the exchange rate between the yen and the dollar: between 1995 and 1997 the yen, which had rather mysteriously gone to sky-high levels, fell back to earth. Since most Asian currencies were more or less pegged to the dollar, this made their exports look more expensive both in Japanese markets and in competition with Japanese products elsewhere, contributing to an export slowdown. China's

1994 devaluation, and more broadly growing competition from China's cheap labor, likewise cut into Thai and Malaysian exports. And there was a worldwide slump in the demand for electronics in general and semiconductors in particular, an area in which Asia's economies had tended to specialize.

But Asia had shrugged off much bigger shocks before. The 1985 crash in oil prices, for example, was a major blow to oil-exporting Indonesia; yet the economy grew right through the bad news. The 1990–91 recession, which was not very severe but affected much of the industrial world, reduced the demand for Asia's exports but did not slow the region's momentum at all. So the important question is, What had changed about Asia (or perhaps the world) such that *these* pieces of bad news triggered an economic avalanche?

Some of the Asians, notably Malaysia's Prime Minister Mahathir, had a ready answer: conspiracy. Mahathir, indeed, argued not only that the panic in Asia was deliberately engineered by big financial operators like George Soros but also that Soros himself was acting on instructions from the U.S. government, which wanted to cut assertive Asians down to size. As time passed, Mahathir's demonization of hedge funds started to look a bit less silly than it did when he first began his ranting. Indeed, the role of hedge funds now looks important enough to rate a whole chapter in this book (Chapter 6). But that role became important mainly in 1998 (by which time, incidentally, the activities of Soros and others were very much contrary to U.S. policy wishes); as a story about how the crisis began, conspiracy theory doesn't wash.

On the other side, many Westerners have turned the story of Asia's crash into a sort of morality play, in which the economies received their inevitable punishment for the sins of crony capitalism. After the catastrophe, everyone had a story about the excesses and corruption of the region—about those finance companies, about Malaysia's grandiose plans for a "technology corridor," about the fortunes made by Suharto's family, about the bizarre diversification of Korean conglomerates (did you hear the one about the underwear company that bought a ski resort, and eventually had to sell it to Michael Jackson?). But this morality play is problematic on at least two counts.

First, while cronyism and corruption were very real in Asia, they were nothing new. Korea's *chaebol* were essentially family enterprises disguised as modern corporations whose owners had been accustomed to special treatment for decades—preferred access to credit, to import licenses, to government subsidies. And those were decades of spectacular economic growth. It was not a pretty system by Western standards but it functioned very well for thirty-five years. The same may be said, to a lesser extent, of all the countries caught up in the crisis. Why did their flaws become crucial only in 1997?

And a related point: if the crisis was a punishment for the sins of the Asian economies, why did economies that were by no means equally far down the path of development all hit the wall at the same time? Korea in 1997 was not far short of being a developed nation, with per capita income comparable to that of southern European countries, while Indonesia was still a very poor country where progress could be measured in terms of how many calories people managed to consume in a day. How is it that such an ill-matched pair could simultaneously be plunged into crisis?

The only answer that makes sense to me, at least, is that the crisis was *not* (mainly) a punishment for sins. There were real failings in these economies, but the main failing was a vulnerability to self-fulfilling panic.

Back to bank runs: In 1931, about half the banks in the United States failed. These banks were not all alike. Some were very badly run; some took excessive risks, even given what they knew before 1929; others were reasonably well, even conservatively managed. But when panic spread across the land, and depositors everywhere wanted their money immediately, none of this mattered: only banks that had been extremely conservative, that had kept what in normal times would be an excessively large share of their deposits in cash, survived. Similarly, Thailand had a badly run economy; it had borrowed far too much and invested it in very dubious projects. Indonesia, for all its corruption, was much less culpable, and truly had the virtues those wise men imagined, but in the panic those distinctions did not matter.

Were the Asian economies more vulnerable to financial panic in 1997 than they had been, say, five or ten years before? Yes, surely—but not because of crony capitalism, or indeed what would usually be considered bad government policies. Rather, they had become more vulnerable partly because they had opened up their financial markets—because they had, in fact, become better free-market economies, not worse. And they had also grown vulnerable because they had taken advantage of their new popularity with international lenders to run up substantial debts to the outside world. These debts intensified the feedback from loss of confidence to financial collapse and back again, making the vicious circle of crisis more intense. It wasn't that the money was badly spent; some of it was, some of it wasn't. It was that the new debts, unlike the old ones, were in dollars—and that turned out to be the economies' undoing.

Epilogue: Argentina, 2002

Argentina isn't an Asian country. (Duh.) But Argentina had an Asian-style crisis in 2002, one that offered a painfully clear demon-

stration of how widely praised economic policies can lead a nation
into disaster.

I discussed Argentina's monetary history in Chapter 2. After
generations of irresponsible use and abuse of the printing press,
in 1991 the Argentine government tried to put an end to all that
by establishing a currency board that would supposedly provide a
permanent link between the Argentine peso and the U.S. dollar.
Every peso in circulation was supposed to be backed by a dollar in
reserves, with no room for discretion. And this monetary stability,
it was hoped, would ensure continued prosperity.

As we saw in Chapter 2, Argentina had a close brush with disaster in 1995, when the backwash from Mexico's crisis came close to
bringing down the banking system. But as that crisis ebbed, confidence returned. Foreign observers continued to shower high praise
on the Argentine economy and its managers, and foreign capital
flowed in, much of it in the form of dollar loans to Argentine businesses and individuals.

In the late 1990s, it all started to go wrong.

At first, the problem was the rigidity of the exchange rate system, which set one peso equal to one U.S. dollar. This might not
have been much of a problem if Argentina, like Mexico, did the
great bulk of its trade with the United States. But look at a map:
Argentina is no closer to the United States than it is to Europe,
and in fact Argentina does more trade both with the European
Union and with its neighbor Brazil than it does with the United
States. And Argentina's currency system did *not* ensure stable
exchange rates against either the euro or the *real*, Brazil's currency.
On the contrary, the system actually tended to cause gratuitous
fluctuations in these exchange rates, and hence in Argentina's
trade position. If, for example, the dollar rose against the euro,

for whatever reason the effect was to price Argentine exports out
of European markets.

And that's exactly what happened to Argentina starting in the
late 1990s. On one side, the dollar soared against the euro—at
one point the euro was worth only $0.85, compared with $1.26
at the time of writing. On the other, Brazil, caught in contagion
from Russia's financial crisis (see Chapter 6), sharply devalued the
real. The combined effect of these exchange rate shifts was to leave
Argentina's exports seriously uncompetitive, pushing the country
into a recession.

As Argentina's economy slumped, foreign investors lost faith.
The flow of capital into the country went into reverse, creating a
credit crunch. And as in 1995, the loss of foreign funds also caused
a banking crisis.

Argentine officials tried desperately to contain the growing crisis. They slashed spending, deepening the recession, in the hope
of regaining investor confidence abroad. They limited withdrawals
from the banks, a measure that provoked angry demonstrations outside the presidential palace, with housewives banging pots and pans.
Nothing seemed to work. And in late 2001 the government found
itself unable to maintain the one-peso-one-dollar rule. The value of
an Argentine peso quickly fell from one dollar to about thirty cents.

The initial results of the currency plunge were catastrophic, just
like the currency plunges in Asia. Since many Argentine businesses
and individuals had debts in dollars, the rise in the cost of a dollar
in pesos had a crippling effect on balance sheets, in many cases
leading to bankruptcy. The economy fell into a swoon: real GDP
fell 11 percent in 2002, after falling 4 percent in 2001. Overall, the
size of the Argentine economy declined 18 percent between 1998
and 2002, a Great Depression–scale contraction.

Over the next five years Argentina made a strong recovery, helped by a settlement in which the government paid only about thirty cents on the dollar of its foreign debt. (One of my favorite headlines ever, from a Reuters report on the debt negotiations, was "Argentina to Creditors: So Sue Us.") But the experience was terrifying. And as this book went to press, Argentina was in crisis again.

The Deeper Question

Most commentators on the Asian crisis would probably find some detail of the account in this chapter to quarrel with. Some would argue that the damage done by moral hazard–driven lending was greater than I suggest. Some would argue, on the contrary, that the economies were really in very good shape, and that the crisis was wholly gratuitous. The precise mechanism of crisis—the respective roles of bank failures, real estate prices, exchange rates, interest rates, and so on—will be the subject of much wrangling for years, perhaps decades to come. Nonetheless, in a general sense I believe that this account would receive broad acceptance.

The real controversy—the one that is heated and often personal, because those who criticize the way the crisis was handled are also criticizing those who handled it—concerns policy. Why weren't governments able to do more to limit the damage?

5

POLICY PERVERSITY

In December 1930, just as it started to become obvious that the United States was in no ordinary recession, John Maynard Keynes attempted to explain the causes of the slump to the general public. "We have magneto [alternator] trouble," he declared. It was, in a way, a radical statement, for he was declaring that the economic engine would not restart of its own accord, that it needed a jump start from the government. But in a deeper sense Keynes was being a conservative: he was declaring that the trouble with the engine was not fundamental, that it was amenable to a technical fix. At a time when many of the world's intellectuals were convinced that capitalism was a failed system, that only by moving to a centrally planned economy could the West emerge from the Great Depression, Keynes was saying that capitalism was *not* doomed, that a very limited sort of intervention—intervention that would leave private property and private decision making intact—was all that was needed to make the system work.

Confounding the skeptics, capitalism did survive; but although today's free-market enthusiasts may find this proposition hard to accept, that survival was basically on the terms Keynes suggested. World War II provided the jump start Keynes had been urging for years; but what restored faith in free markets was not just the recovery from the Depression but the assurance that macroeconomic intervention—cutting interest rates or increasing budget deficits to fight recessions—could keep a free-market economy more or less stable at more or less full employment. In effect, capitalism and its economists made a deal with the public: it will be okay to have free markets from now on, because we know enough to prevent any more Great Depressions.

This implicit deal actually has a name: in the 1950s Paul Samuelson, in his famous textbook, called it the "neoclassical synthesis." But I prefer to think of it as the "Keynesian compact."

In the United States and most other advanced countries, that compact is still honored. Oh, there are recessions now and then. However, when they occur, everyone expects the Federal Reserve to do what it did in 1975, 1982, and 1991: cut interest rates to perk up the economy. And we also expect the president and Congress to cut taxes and raise spending if necessary to help the process. We surely do not expect that a recession will be met, Herbert Hoover style, by raising taxes, cutting spending, and increasing interest rates.

But when financial disaster struck Asia, the policies those countries followed in response were almost exactly the reverse of what the United States has done in the face of a slump. Fiscal austerity was the order of the day; interest rates were increased, often to punitive levels. This was not because the policymakers in those countries were stupid or ill informed. On the contrary, for the most part they understood the Keynesian compact very well, indeed had tried to adhere to it in the past. Anyway, once the crisis struck, Asian countries found their policies largely dictated by Washington—that is, by the International Monetary Fund and the U.S. Treasury. And the leadership of those institutions was extremely sophisticated: one could argue that never in history had so many first-rate economists been in positions of so much authority.

Why did these extremely clever men advocate policies for emerging market economies that were completely perverse in terms of standard economic doctrine? The short answer is "fear of speculators." But that short answer makes sense only if put into context—specifically, if we spend some time trying to understand the dilemmas of international money.

How the International Monetary System Didn't Evolve

Once upon a time, the world had a single currency, the globo. It was well managed: the Global Reserve Bank (popularly known as the Glob), under its chairman Alan Globespan, did a reasonably good job of increasing the global money supply when the world threatened to slide into recession, and trimming it when there were indications of inflation. Indeed, in later years some would remember the reign of the globo as a golden age. Businessmen in particular liked the system because they could buy and sell anywhere with a minimum of hassle.

But there was trouble in paradise. You see, although careful management of the globo could prevent a boom-bust cycle *for the world as a whole*, it could not do so for each piece of that whole. Indeed, it turned out that there were often conflicts of interest about monetary policy. Sometimes the Glob would be following an easy-money policy because Europe and Asia were on the edge of recession; but that easy money would fuel a wild speculative boom in North America. At other times the Glob would feel obliged to tighten money to head off inflation in North America, intensifying a developing recession in South America. And because there were no separate continental currencies, there was nothing continental governments could do about these problems.

Eventually there came a time when the frustrations grew too great, and the system broke up. Instead of the globo, each continent introduced its own currency and proceeded to pursue monetary policies tailored to its own needs. When Europe's economy was overheating, it could reduce the supply of euros; when Latin America slumped, it could increase the supply of latinos. The awkwardness of a one-size-fits-all monetary policy was gone.

But it soon turned out that disposing of one problem created another because the exchange rates between continental currencies fluctuated wildly. One might have thought that the exchange rate between, say, the latino and the euro would be determined by the needs of trade: by Latin Americans trading latinos for euros in order to buy European goods, and conversely. It soon became clear, however, that the market was dominated mainly by investors— people buying and selling currencies in order to purchase stocks and bonds. And since these investment demands were highly variable, including a large component of speculation, currency values also proved unstable. Worse yet, people began to speculate on the values of the currencies themselves. The result was that exchange rates bounced around, creating uncertainty for businesses, which could never be sure what their overseas assets and liabilities were really worth.

So some continents tried to stabilize exchange rates—buying

and selling on the foreign exchange market in order to keep the price of a euro in terms of afros, or a gringo in terms of latinos, constant. Central banks reserved the right, however, to change the target exchange rates if necessary—say, by devaluing their currency if this seemed necessary to fight unemployment.

Alas, this "adjustable peg" system turned out to offer speculators too many easy targets: when a continent experienced economic difficulties, and started to look as if it might consider a devaluation, speculators would begin selling its currency in anticipation. This would soon force the continental central bank either to raise interest rates, actually worsening the slump, or to devalue immediately. Or—the one remaining option—it could try to defeat the speculators directly, by placing restrictions on the movement of capital.

And so the world's continents were forced into choosing one of three "currency regimes," each of which had a serious defect. They could opt to maintain an independent monetary policy and let the exchange rate fluctuate as it pleased; this left them free to fight recessions, but introduced disturbing uncertainty into business life. They could fix the value of the exchange rate and attempt to convince markets that they would never devalue; this would make business life simpler and safer but would bring back the problem of one-size-fits-all monetary policy. Or they could continue to maintain an adjustable peg, that is, fix the exchange rate but retain the option of changing it; but this was workable only if they maintained controls on capital movement, which were hard to enforce, imposed extra costs on business, and—like any prohibition on potentially profitable transactions—were a source of corruption.

Okay, okay, it didn't really happen quite that way. There never was a globo; the closest thing to it was the pre-1930s gold standard, which unfortunately was *not* managed so as to prevent worldwide booms and busts. But our imaginary history does illustrate a bit more clearly than the complexities of what actually happened the three-cornered dilemma, or "trilemma," that national economies face in a global economy.

Think of it this way. There are three things that macroeconomic managers want for their economies. They want discretion in monetary policy so that they can fight recessions and curb inflation. They want stable exchange rates so that businesses are not faced with too much uncertainty. And they want to leave international business free—in particular, to allow people to exchange money however they like—in order to get out of the private sector's way.

What the story of the globo and its demise tells us is that countries cannot get all three wishes; at most, they can get two. They can give up on exchange rate stability; this means adopting a floating exchange rate, like the United States and Australia did. They can give up on discretionary monetary policy; this means fixing the exchange rate, the way Argentina did in the 1990s, and possibly even giving up their own currency, like the nations of continental Europe did. Or they can give up on the principle of completely free markets and impose capital controls; this was what most countries did between the 1940s and the 1960s, and what China does right now.

Which of these three imperfect answers is best? There are some people who think that the gains from stable exchange rates are large, the benefits of independent monetary policy overrated. They like to point out that the United States, though spread over a continent, does very well with a single currency, and that some 300 million Europeans have adopted a common currency. So why not the world as a whole? But most economists will point out that the United States has special features that help it live with a single currency: most notably, workers can and do move rapidly from depressed to booming regions, so that one size of monetary policy more or less does fit all. The introduction of the euro, Europe's currency, was in fact quite controversial, with many economists questioning whether Europe is anywhere near as suited to a single money as the United States. But at least the major European economies are rather similar to each other and very closely linked, so that most of the time a monetary policy that is appropriate for France will also be appropriate for Germany, and vice versa. It is hard to see, however, how a suitable monetary policy could be devised that is appropriate for both Japan and the United States, let alone the United States and Argentina. So relatively few economists are nostalgic for the days of the gold standard, or fantasize about the coming of the globo; national, or perhaps regional, monetary independence is still needed.

On the other hand, the capital controls that allowed advanced countries to combine fixed exchange rates with Keynesian policies in the first postwar generation are now very much out of fashion. The fundamental problem with these controls is that the distinction between "good" and "bad" international transactions is a hard one to make. A speculator who pulls his money out of Malaysia because he is trying to profit from a devaluation is engaged in an antisocial act; a Malaysian exporter who wins customers abroad in part by letting them buy now, pay later is helping the country earn its way in world markets. But suppose that the exporter, suspecting that the ringgit will soon be devalued, asks his customers to pay in dollars and encourages them to take a long time before settling. The effect is the same as if he took ringgit and bought dollars on the black market. And there are dozens of other ways in which the line between productive business and currency speculation can be blurred. What this means is either that attempts to control speculation will be easily evaded or that the government can limit speculation only by imposing onerous restrictions on ordinary transactions (e.g., limiting the credit exporters can give their customers). Fifty years ago most governments regarded these restrictions as a price worth paying. Today, however, we live in a world that has relearned the virtues of free markets, is suspicious of government intervention, and is particularly aware that the more things are prohibited, the greater the scope for bribery and cronyism.

Which leaves freely floating exchange rates, which by the mid-1990s most economists had come to regard as the lesser of three evils. True, exchange rates have repeatedly proved to be far more volatile than they "should" be, given economic fundamentals (over the past fifteen years the dollar-yen rate has gone from 120, to 80, to nearly 150, then back below 110, all with relatively little measurable change in fundamentals); and even those who are generally pro-floating agree that tightly integrated regions that form "optimal currency areas" should adopt the ultimate form of fixed exchange rates, a common currency. (Whether Europe constitutes such an area is another question.) But as a general rule, the preferred alternative of most economists—and, in particular, the one most consistent with the Keynesian compact, because it leaves countries free to pursue both free-market and full-employment policies—is a floating exchange rate.

The virtues of such free floating, when it works, are not hard to demonstrate. The United States is well served by its general policy of benign neglect toward the foreign exchange value of the dollar; while the dollar-yen and dollar-euro rates may go through annoying gyrations, this annoyance is surely a small thing compared with the freedom of action the absence of an exchange rate commitment gives to the Federal Reserve—the ability to cut interest rates sharply and immediately when recession or financial crisis looms.

Better yet, consider the example of Australia during the Asian crisis. In 1996 an Australian dollar was worth almost eighty cents in U.S. currency. By the late summer of 1998 it had fallen to little more than sixty cents. No surprise there: most of Australia's exports went either to Japan or to the troubled tigers. But Australia, except for a brief period in the summer of 1998 when it seemed to be facing a coordinated attack by hedge funds (more on that in the next chapter), did not try to prop up its currency, either by buying it on the foreign exchange market or by raising interest rates. Instead, the currency's fall proved self-limiting: when the Aussie dollar fell, investors regarded it as an opportunity to invest cheaply in what they continued to regard as a solid economy. And this confidence appeared justified by the "Australian miracle": despite its dependence on Asian markets, Australia actually boomed amidst Asia's crisis.

But if Australia could so easily avoid getting caught up in its neighbors' economic catastrophe, why couldn't Indonesia or South Korea do the same?

The Speculative Threat

Imagine an economy that isn't perfect. (What economy is?) Maybe the government is running a budget deficit that, while not really threatening its solvency, is coming down more slowly than it should, or maybe banks with political connections have made too many loans to questionable borrowers. But, as far as anyone can tell from the numbers, there are no problems that cannot be dealt with given goodwill and a few years of stability.

Then, for some reason—perhaps an economic crisis on the other side of the world—investors become jittery and start pulling their money out en masse. Suddenly the country is in trouble—its stock market is plunging, its interest rates are soaring. You might think that savvy investors would see this as an opportunity to buy. After all, if the fundamentals haven't changed, doesn't this mean that assets are now undervalued? But, as we saw in Chapter 4, the answer is "not necessarily." The crash in asset values may cause previously sound banks to collapse. Economic slump, high interest rates, and a devalued exchange rate may cause sound companies to go bankrupt. At worst, economic distress may cause political instability. Maybe buying when everyone else is rushing for the exits isn't such a good idea after all; maybe it's better to run for the exit yourself.

Thus it is possible in principle that a loss of confidence in a country can produce an economic crisis that justifies that loss of confidence—that countries may be vulnerable to what economists call "self-fulfilling speculative attacks." And while many economists used to be skeptical about the importance of such self-fulfilling crises, the experience of the 1990s in Latin America and Asia settled those doubts, at least as a practical matter.

The funny thing is that once you take the possibility of self-fulfilling crises seriously, market psychology becomes crucial—so crucial that within limits, the expectations, even the prejudices of investors, become economic fundamentals—because believing makes it so.

Suppose, for example, that everyone is convinced that despite its remarkably high dependence on foreign capital (it has run large current account deficits of more than 4 percent of GDP for decades), Australia is basically a sound country—it can be counted on to be politically and economically stable. Then the market response to a decline in the Australian dollar is in effect to say, "Good, that's over, let's buy Australian," and the economy actually benefits. The market's good opinion is therefore confirmed.

On the other hand, suppose that despite twenty years of remarkable progress people are not quite convinced that Indonesia is no longer the country of *The Year of Living Dangerously*. Then when the rupiah falls they may say, "Oh, my God, they're reverting to the bad old days"; the resulting capital flight leads to financial, economic, and political crisis, and the market's bad opinion is similarly confirmed.

It seems, in other words, that the Keynesian compact is a sometime thing. The common view among economists that floating rates are the best, if imperfect, solution to the international monetary trilemma was based on the experience of countries like Canada, Britain, and the United States. But during the 1990s a series of countries—Mexico, Thailand, Indonesia, Korea—discovered that they were subject to different rules. Again and again, attempts to engage in moderate devaluations led to a drastic collapse in confidence. It is this problem of confidence that ultimately explains why the Keynesian compact has been broken.

The Confidence Game

In the summer of 1998 Brazil was already suffering an economic slowdown; unemployment was rising, while inflation—Brazil's traditional ailment—had given way to price stability, and some were even talking of deflation. Then the collapse of economic reform in Russia triggered an attack on Brazil's *real* (why? See Chapter 6), and the country went to the United States and the IMF for help. What Brazil wanted was both money and, even more important, a sort of Good Housekeeping seal on its policies, something that would persuade nervous investors to stop running. In return, it promised to implement a program of economic "stabilization."

So what did the program—intended, remember, for a country with a slowing economy and no inflation to speak of—involve? Higher taxes, reduced government spending, and a continuation of extremely high interest rates (Brazil had raised rates to nearly

50 percent when the crisis began). In other words, the Brazilian government implemented extremely tight monetary and fiscal policies, which guaranteed that the country would experience a nasty recession in 1999.

The program for Brazil was peculiarly extreme; it was almost like a caricature of the policies that had been introduced in Asia the preceding year. But like many caricatures, it emphasized the distinctive features of its subject. At the core of the policies imposed by Washington on many of the crisis countries was an almost perfect inversion of the Keynesian compact: faced with an economic crisis, countries were urged to raise interest rates, slash spending, and increase taxes.

Why, sixty years after Keynes, would anybody think that it was a good idea to break so profoundly with the Keynesian compact? The answer lay in the perceived need to win market confidence at all costs.

First of all, the Australian solution—just letting the currency slide—was ruled out. The fixed exchange rate between Brazil's *real* and the dollar had been a centerpiece of the country's reform program, the program that had brought price stability after generations of high inflation. To give up that fixed rate, both Brazil and Washington feared, would be devastating for investor confidence. True, one could make a good case that the *real* was, say, 20 percent overvalued and that a 20 percent devaluation would do the country far more good than harm. But nobody believed that a 20 percent devaluation was a realistic strategy: as one U.S. official put it, "For developing countries, there are no small devaluations."

How was a devaluation of the *real* to be avoided? The IMF could supply money, which together with the country's own foreign exchange reserves could be used to support the currency in the markets. But this money would soon be gone unless something could be done to stop capital flight. The only tool immediately at hand was to impose very high interest rates, high enough to persuade people to keep money in Brazil even though they suspected that its currency might end up devalued after all.

Nor was that all. When the markets decided that Brazil was a bad risk, they also decided that at the core of Brazil's problems was its large budget deficit. Now, you could question that assessment. Brazil's government actually didn't have all that much debt—considerably less, as a share of national income, than many European countries or Japan. And much of the deficit was actually a consequence of the crisis: high interest rates had driven up the government's interest payments, while the slumping economy depressed tax revenue. (At "normal" levels of employment and interest rates, Brazil's budget deficit would have been quite modest.) But what was the use of arguing? Investors believed that Brazil would have a disastrous crisis unless the deficit was quickly reduced, and they were surely right, because they themselves would generate that crisis. (And indeed they did, in January 1999.)

The point is that because speculative attacks can be self-justifying, following an economic policy that makes sense in terms of the fundamentals is not enough to assure market confidence. In fact, the need to win that confidence can actually prevent a country from following otherwise sensible policies and force it to follow policies that would normally seem perverse.

Now, consider the situation from the point of view of those clever economists who were making policy in Washington. They found themselves dealing with economies whose hold on investor confidence was fragile. Almost by definition a country that has come to the United States and/or the IMF for help is one that has already experienced a devastating run on its currency and is at risk of another. The overriding objective of policy must therefore be to mollify market sentiment. But because crises can be self-fulfilling, sound economic policy is not sufficient to gain market confidence—one must cater to the perceptions, the prejudices, the whims of the market. Or, rather, one must cater to what one *hopes* will be the perceptions of the market.

And that is how the Keynesian compact got broken: international economic policy ended up having very little to do with economics. It became an exercise in amateur psychology, in which the IMF and the Treasury Department tried to persuade countries to do things they hoped would be perceived by the market as favorable. No wonder the economics textbooks went right out the window as soon as the crisis hit.

Unfortunately, the textbook issues did not go away. Suppose that Washington was right, that a country threatened with an investor panic must raise interest rates, cut spending, and defend its currency to avoid devastating crisis. It still remains true that tight monetary and fiscal policies, together with an overvalued currency, produce recessions. What remedy does Washington offer? None. The perceived need to play the confidence game supersedes the normal concerns of economic policy. It sounds pretty crazy, and it is.

And so now we have solved the mystery with which Chapter 4 ended: why did policy fail to oppose the devastating feedback process that caused one economy after another to melt down? The answer is that those making policy believed that they had to play the confidence game, and that this meant following macroeconomic policies that exacerbated slumps instead of relieving them.

But was it really necessary to play this game?

Did the IMF Make the Situation Worse?

Nobody likes the International Monetary Fund; if anyone did, it would be a bad sign. For the IMF is a "lender of last resort" for national governments: it is the place they go for money when they are in trouble. And lenders of last resort are supposed to practice tough love: to give you what you need rather than what you want, and to force you to pull yourself together in the process. A warm, cuddly IMF wouldn't be doing its job.

But the converse isn't necessarily true: just because people hate the IMF doesn't mean that it is doing its job well. And since the onset of the Asian crisis there have been many complaints about the IMF's role. Quite a few people think that the IMF (and the U.S. Treasury Department, which de facto largely dictates the IMF's policies) actually caused the crisis, or that it mishandled the crisis in a way that made it far worse than it needed to be. Are they right?

Let's start with the easy part: two things that the IMF clearly did do wrong.

First, when the IMF was called in to Thailand, Indonesia, and Korea, it quickly demanded that they practice fiscal austerity—that they raise taxes and cut spending in order to avoid large budget deficits. It was hard to understand why this was part of the program, since in Asia (unlike in Brazil a year later) nobody but the IMF seemed to regard budget deficits as an important problem. And the attempt to meet these budget guidelines had a doubly negative effect on the countries: where the guidelines were met, the effect was to worsen the recession by reducing demand; where they were not met, the effect was to add, gratuitously, to the sense that things were out of control, and hence to feed the market panic.

Second, the IMF demanded "structural" reform—that is, changes that went well beyond monetary and fiscal policy—as a condition for loans to afflicted economies. Some of these reforms, like closing bad banks, were arguably relevant to the financial crisis. Others, like demanding that Indonesia eliminate the practice of giving presidential cronies lucrative monopolies in some businesses, had little if anything to do with the IMF's mandate. True, the monopoly on cloves (which Indonesians like to put in their cigarettes) was a bad thing, a glaring example of crony capitalism at work. But what did it have to do with the run on the rupiah?

If you had asked IMF officials at the time what they thought they were doing, they would have answered that it was all part of the business of rebuilding confidence. Budget deficits were not a market concern at the moment, but they thought they soon would be. And they also thought that it was important for countries to make a highly visible show of combating cronyism and corruption, to convince markets that they really had changed their ways. One might almost describe this as the view that governments had to show their seriousness by inflicting pain on themselves—whether or not that pain had any direct relevance to the immediate problems—because only thus could they regain the market's trust.

If that was the theory, it turns out to have been quite wrong. The budget guidelines were eventually relaxed, and nobody minded; markets became bullish once again on Korea, even though structural reform had stalled. Meanwhile, the sheer breadth of IMF demands, aside from raising suspicions that the United States was trying to use the crisis to impose its ideological vision on Asia, more or less guaranteed a prolonged period of wrangling between Asian governments and their rescuers, a period during which the crisis of confidence steadily worsened.

So the IMF bungled two important pieces of the rescue. But the really big issues involved interest rates and exchange rates. Did it bungle these too?

Here's what the IMF did: In Asia (as opposed to Brazil, which as I said was a sort of caricature of the Asian programs) it did not tell countries to defend the values of their currencies at all cost. But it did tell them to raise interest rates, initially to very high levels, in an attempt to persuade investors to keep their money in place. Some vociferous critics of the IMF—most notably Harvard's Jeffrey Sachs—said that this was very much the wrong thing to do. Sachs believed, in effect, that Asian countries could and should have behaved like Australia, simply letting their currencies decline until they started to look cheap to investors, and that if they had done so, the great slump would never have happened.

What the IMF said in response is that Asia is not Australia: that to let the currencies fall unchecked would have led to "hyperdevaluations," and that the result would have been both massive financial distress (because so many businesses had debt denominated in dollars) and soaring inflation. The trouble with this rationale is, of course, that the massive financial distress happened anyway, thanks to high interest rates and the recession they helped cause. So the IMF at best avoided one vicious circle only by starting another.

This same observation undermines the argument made by many right-wing critics of the IMF, that it *should* have told countries to defend their original exchange rates at all cost. This could indeed have avoided the collapse of confidence in Asian *currencies*; but it would have done nothing to prevent the collapse of confidence in Asian *economies*, and the economic meltdown would probably still have happened.

Would simply letting the currencies fall have worked better? Sachs argued that by *not* raising interest rates, governments would have avoided feeding the financial panic; the result would have been modest, tolerable devaluations and a far better economic outcome. This argument, which seemed implausible to many people (myself included) at the time of the Asian crisis, gained a bit more credibility in January 1999, when Washington quite clearly bungled Brazil—but more about that in Chapter 7.

Surely, however, the bottom line is that there were no good choices. The rules of the international financial system, it seemed, offered many countries no way out. And so it was really nobody's fault that things turned out so badly.

Which is not to say that there were no villains in the plot.

6

MASTERS OF THE UNIVERSE

In the bad old days, before the triumph of capitalism, the figure of the evil speculator—the malefactor of great wealth who manipulates markets to the detriment of honest workers—was a staple of popular culture. But with the fall of Communism, the successes of globalization, and the general revival of faith in free markets, the evil speculator went the way of witches and warlocks: serious people stopped believing in his existence. Oh, nobody but the most extreme defenders of laissez-faire denied that there were cases in which people traded on inside information and maybe even manipulated the price of a stock here, a commodity there. But surely this was petty crime; the big financial events, those that shaped the destiny of nations, involved markets far too large for conspiracy theories to be plausible. No individuals or small groups could really affect the currency value of even a middle-sized economy, could they?

Well, maybe they could. One of the most bizarre aspects of the economic crisis of the 1990s was the prominent part played by "hedge funds," investment institutions that are able to take temporary control of assets far in excess of their owners' wealth. Without question hedge funds, in both their success and their failure, rocked world markets. And in at least a few cases, the evil speculator staged a comeback.

The Nature of the Beast

Hedge funds don't hedge. Indeed, they do more or less the opposite. To hedge, says *Webster's*, is "to try to avoid or lessen loss by making counterbalancing bets, investments, etc." That is, one hedges in order to make sure that market fluctuations do *not* affect one's wealth.

What hedge funds do, by contrast, is precisely to try to make the most of market fluctuations. The way they do this is typically to go short in some assets—that is, promise to deliver them at a fixed price at some future date—and go long in others. Profits come if the price of the shorted asset falls (so that they can be delivered cheaply) or the value of the purchased asset rises, or both.*

---

* The terminology of "short" versus "long" positions is jargon, but too useful a shorthand to be avoided in this book. Basically, to go long in something is to put yourself in a position to gain if its price rises—which is what the ordinary investor does when buying stock, real estate, or anything else. To go short in something is to put yourself in a position to gain if its price *falls*. To sell a stock short, one borrows the stock from its owner with a promise to return it later—then one sells it. This means that the stock must be repurchased before the due date; the short-seller is betting that its price will have fallen by then. Meanwhile, the short-seller has acquired extra cash, which can be invested in something else—that is, he takes a long position in some other asset.

Of course, the owners of the borrowed assets have to be reassured that the short-seller will actually have enough cash to buy the asset back, so they will want some kind

The advantage of this kind of financial play is that it can deliver a very high return to the hedge fund's investors. The reason is that the fund can take a position much larger than the amount of money its owners put in, since it buys its "long" position mainly with the cash raised from creating its "short" position. Indeed, the only reason it needs to have any capital at all is to persuade the counterparties to its asset shorts that it will be able to deliver on its promises. Hedge funds with good reputations have been able to take positions as much as a hundred times as large as their owners' capital; that means that a 1 percent rise in the price of their assets, or decline in the price of their liabilities, doubles that capital.

The downside, of course, is that a hedge fund can also lose money very efficiently. Market movements that might not seem all that large to ordinary investors can quickly wipe out a hedge fund's capital, or at least cause it to lose its shorts—that is, induce those who have lent it stocks or other assets to demand that they be returned.

How big are hedge funds? Nobody really knows because until quite recently nobody thought it was necessary to find out. Indeed, despite occasional warnings from concerned economists, and even despite the events I'll describe shortly, hedge funds have been left virtually untouched by regulation. Partly that's because hedge funds—needing only a limited amount of capital, from a small number of people—can and do operate "offshore," establishing legal residence in accommodating jurisdictions to free themselves

---

of reassurance that he has enough wealth to deliver on his promise. When investors who engage in a lot of short-selling suffer heavy losses, they typically find that they are no longer able to borrow as much as they could before. When such investors play a large role in the market, this can have interesting consequences, as we will see shortly.

from annoying interference. To police their operations wouldn't be impossible, but it would be difficult. Moreover, for a long time the general consensus, at least in the United States, was that there was no need.

But in a way that was a strange attitude, because as early as 1992 one famous hedge fund gave an impressive demonstration of just how much influence a highly leveraged investor can have.

The Legend of George Soros

George Soros, a Hungarian refugee turned American entrepreneur, founded his Quantum Fund in 1969. By 1992 he was a billionaire, already famous as the "world's greatest investor," and already celebrated for the generosity and creativity of his philanthropic activities. But Soros—who is a man with intellectual as well as financial ambitions, who would like the world to take his philosophical pronouncements as seriously as it takes his business acumen—wanted more. As he himself says, he went in search of a business coup that would not only make money but generate publicity for himself, publicity that he could use to promote his nonbusiness ventures.

He found his opportunity in Britain that summer. In 1990 Britain had joined the European Monetary System's Exchange Rate Mechanism (ERM), a system of fixed exchange rates that was intended as a way station en route to a unified European currency. Like the unhappy continents in our globo parable, however, Britain found that it did not like the monetary policy it was forced to follow. At the time Europe did not have a European Central Bank; while there was a legal fiction of symmetry among nations, in practice everyone matched the monetary policy of Germany's Bundesbank. And Germany was, literally, in a different place from the rest of Europe: having just reunified, it was compelled to spend large sums on the attempted reconstruction of East Germany. Fearing that this expenditure would be inflationary, the Bundesbank maintained high interest rates to prevent its own economy from overheating. Meanwhile Britain, which probably entered the ERM at too high an exchange rate, was in a deep recession, and its government was facing growing popular dissatisfaction. Officials strenuously denied that they would consider dropping out of the ERM; but there was a nagging doubt about whether they really meant it.

It was a situation ready-made for a currency crisis, and Soros decided not only to bet on such a crisis but also to provoke one.

The mechanics of the bet were conceptually simple, if extremely complex in detail. The first stage had to be low profile, even secretive, as the Quantum Fund quietly established credit lines that would allow it to borrow about $15 billion worth of British pounds and to convert that sum into dollars at will. Then, once the fund was already substantially long in dollars and short in pounds, the attack had to turn noisy: Soros would be as ostentatious as possible about short-selling the pound, give interviews to financial newspapers declaring his belief that the pound would soon be devalued, and so on. If all went well, this would generate a run on the pound by other investors, a run that would force the British government to give in and devalue it.

It worked. Soros's high-profile assault on the pound began in August. Within weeks Britain had spent nearly $50 billion in the foreign exchange markets to defend the pound, to no avail. In mid-September the government raised interest rates to defend the currency, but this proved politically unacceptable. After only three days Britain dropped out of the ERM, and the pound was set afloat (where it remains to this day). Soros not only made roughly a billion dollars in quick capital gains but also established himself as perhaps the most famous speculator of all time.

But what did Soros actually do? There are three questions here.

First, did Soros undermine a currency that would otherwise have maintained its value? Probably not. The fact is that pressures on the pound were building steadily, and many economists (though not many market participants) already suspected that Britain was not long for the ERM. Nobody can prove this assertion, but my strong belief is that Britain's attempt to join the continental monetary club was doomed, Soros or no Soros.

But in that case, did Soros at least move up the timetable, causing the pound to devalue sooner than it otherwise would have? Almost surely yes, but the question is, by how much? Again, one cannot prove this one way or the other, but my own guess is that economic conditions were moving Britain in the direction of a near-term exit from the ERM in any case and that Soros moved up the timetable by only a few weeks.

Finally, did Soros do his victims any harm? The government of Prime Minister John Major never recovered from the humiliation. But it is actually possible to argue that Soros did the British nation as a whole a favor. The decline of the pound did not create an economic crisis: the currency stabilized spontaneously at about 15 percent below its previous value. Freed of the need to support the pound, the British government was able to reduce interest rates. (Chancellor of the Exchequer Norman Lamont declared that he had been "singing in the bath" with relief over the end of a currency peg he had declared absolutely inviolable only a few days before. His relief was premature—most Britons gained from the devaluation, but he himself was soon forced to resign.) The combination of lower interest rates and a more competitive exchange rate soon led to a strong recovery in the British economy, which within a few years had brought unemployment down to levels its neighbors regarded as unreachable. For the ordinary Briton, Soros's attack on the pound brought mainly good things.

So it wasn't such a terrible story, after all. True, Europeans who were deeply committed to the cause of monetary union regarded the events of 1992 as a tragedy. The French, who basically fought off the speculative attacks of 1992 and 1993 (they briefly allowed the franc to float, but soon brought it back into the ERM band), were heard to mutter old-fashioned denunciations of currency speculators as agents of evil. But in the dominant Anglo-Saxon world of policy discussion, the story of Soros and the pound was not regarded as any sort of worrisome omen.

All that changed when the Asian crisis hit, and it turned out that the results of speculation could be considerably less benign.

The Madness of Prime Minister Mahathir

Try to imagine how it must have felt. He had managed his country's awkward ethnic politics with consummate skill: he pacified the country's Malay majority with the *bumiputra* ("son of the soil") program offering that majority preferential economic treatment, yet did so without driving out the commercially crucial Chinese minority. He had made the nation a favorite site for multinational branch plants even while pursuing an independent, somewhat anti-Western foreign policy that played well with a mostly Islamic populace. And under his leadership the country had shared fully in the Asian miracle: as its economy surged, foreign businessmen, from Bill Gates on down, came courting, and in the summer of 1997 *Time* declared him one of the world's top one hundred "technology leaders."

Oh, there were a few criticisms. Some of his friends and family members seemed to have gotten rich rather easily. Some foreigners accused him of grandiosity, with his insistence on building the world's tallest building and on constructing a new capital and a massive new "technology corridor." But on the whole he had every reason to feel well satisfied with his achievements.

Then, with shocking suddenness, things went sour. His undisciplined neighbors had a currency crisis—well, that was their problem. But then money started flooding out of his country too. He was faced with the humiliating choice between letting the currency plunge or raising interest rates, either of which would put many of those hard-built businesses in severe financial straits.

So in a way we should not blame Mahathir Mohamad, prime minister of Malaysia, for his susceptibility to conspiracy theories. After all, it was common knowledge that George Soros had engineered the run on the pound five years earlier, and Quantum Fund had certainly been speculating in Southeast Asian currencies over the past several years. What was more natural than to blame the famous speculator for his woes? One might even call it a bit of poetic justice: Soros, by his own account, had attacked the pound as much for the notoriety as the money; now he was being hoisted by his own petard.

Nonetheless, Mahathir clearly should have kept his mouth shut. At a time when confidence in his economy was already plunging, the sight of the prime minister raving about an American conspiracy against Asia—and broadly hinting that it was in fact, yes, a *Jewish* conspiracy—was not what the money doctors would have prescribed.

And it also happened not to be true. Quantum Fund had speculated against Thailand, but then so had lots of people. The speculative flight of capital from Malaysia, it turns out, was carried out largely by Malaysians themselves—in particular, some of the very same businessmen who had gotten rich thanks to Mahathir's favor.

Nonetheless, Mahathir continued to press his case, attacking Soros in press conferences and speeches. Only after several months had gone by, and the state of the Malaysian economy began to look truly alarming, did he become relatively quiet, afraid to disturb the markets. Perhaps he also became aware that most of the world thought his complaints were silly. Conspiracies like that just don't happen in the real world.

And then one did.

The Attack on Hong Kong

Hong Kong has long had a special place in the hearts of free-market enthusiasts. At a time when most Third World countries believed that protectionism and government planning were the way to develop, Hong Kong had free trade and a policy of letting entrepreneurs rip—and showed that such a wide-open economy could grow at rates development theorists had never imagined possible. The city-state also led the revival of currency boards, which some conservatives liked to imagine constituted the first step on the road back to the gold standard. Year after year the conservative Heritage Foundation gave Hong Kong top ranking on its "index of economic freedom."

But Hong Kong suffered from the Asian crisis. It is hard to find any fault in the city's own management: more than any other in the region, its economy was run according to the rule of law, with well-regulated banks and conservative budget policies. There was little sign of rampant cronyism before the crisis, nor was there, in the first year, any panicky flight of capital. Still, the city was clearly in the wrong place at the wrong time. As its neighbors slumped, business suffered: Japanese stopped popping over for shopping trips, Southeast Asian firms stopped buying the services of Hong Kong banks. Worse yet, Hong Kong's strict currency board system meant that the exchange rate was fixed solidly at 7.8 to the U.S. dollar, even as much of the rest of Asia's currencies were devalued, and suddenly Hong Kong was far more expensive than Bangkok or even Tokyo. The result was a deepening recession, the worst in memory.

Inevitably, nagging doubts began to surface. Would Hong Kong really defend its exchange rate at all costs? Some Hong Kong businessmen openly urged the Monetary Authority to devalue the currency, to make their costs competitive again. Such demands were dismissed, and the government declared the rate inviolate; but then so had the government of Britain in 1992. Also, what about China? Asia's giant largely escaped the first wave of the crisis, thanks mainly to its currency controls. But by the summer of 1998 signs of an economic slowdown were emerging, and with them rumors that China's currency, too, might be devalued, putting Hong Kong under far greater strain.

Some might have seen all of this as bad news; but some hedge funds saw it as an opportunity.

There are, for obvious reasons, no hard numbers on just what happened in August and September of 1998, but here is the way the story is told, both by Hong Kong officials and by market players. A small group of hedge funds—rumored to include Soros's Quantum Fund and Julian Robertson's less famous but equally influential Tiger Fund, although officials named no names—began a "double play" against Hong Kong. They sold Hong Kong stocks short—that is, they borrowed stocks from their owners, then sold them for Hong Kong dollars (with a promise to those owners to buy the stocks back and return them, of course—as well as a "rental fee" for the use of the stocks in the meantime). Then they traded those Hong Kong dollars for U.S. dollars. In effect, they were betting that one of two things would happen. Either the Hong Kong dollar would be devalued, so that they would make money on their currency speculation; or the Hong Kong Monetary Authority would defend its currency by raising interest rates, which would drive down the local stock market, and they would make money off their stock market short position.

But in the view of Hong Kong officials, the hedge funds weren't just betting on these events: like Soros in 1992, they were doing their best to make them happen. The sales of Hong Kong dollars were ostentatious, carried out in large blocks, regularly timed, so as to make sure that everyone in the market noticed. Again without naming names, Hong Kong officials also claimed that the hedge funds paid reporters and editors to run stories suggesting that the Hong Kong dollar or the Chinese renminbi, or both, were on the verge of devaluation. In other words, they were deliberately trying to start a run on the currency.

Did the hedge funds actually conspire together? It's possible: while an explicit agreement to manipulate the price of, say, Microsoft stock would land you in jail, a comparable conspiracy against the Hong Kong stock market (which had about the same capitalization in 1998) apparently falls through the legal cracks. It's also possible there was no contact at all. But more likely there were hints and winks, a few generalities over a round of golf or an expensive bottle of wine. After all, there weren't that many players, and they all knew how the game worked.

Indeed, some observers saw the shadow of a still wider plot. The

Hong Kong Four (or Five, or whatever) had other plays going at the same time. They were short in yen—because interest rates in Japan were low, and they thought the yen might well plunge along with the Hong Kong dollar—as well as Australian dollars, Canadian dollars, and so on. And they became big, ostentatious sellers of some of these other currencies too. So you could think of Hong Kong as only the centerpiece of a play against much of the Asia-Pacific region, indeed quite possibly the largest market conspiracy of all time.

And it all looked quite likely to succeed. After all, what could Hong Kong do? Its stock market was large compared with that of most developing countries but not compared with the resources of the hedge funds. There were reports that the combined short position of the alleged conspirators was about $30 billion, which would be the equivalent of short-selling roughly $1.5 *trillion* in the U.S. stock market. Moreover, the Hong Kong market was wide open and likely to remain so: a city whose livelihood depended precisely on its reputation as a place where people could do as they liked with their money, free from arbitrary government interference, would not even dare to flirt with controls on capital flight. All in all, it looked like a brilliant plan, with very high chances of success.

Unexpectedly, Hong Kong fought back.

The main weapon in that fight was a novel, unconventional use of the Hong Kong Monetary Authority's funds. The HKMA, as it happened, had huge resources. Remember, Hong Kong had a currency board, so that every 7.8 Hong Kong dollars of money in circulation was backed by one U.S. dollar in reserves; but it turned out that the HKMA had actually banked far more dollars than it needed for that purpose. How could this wealth be deployed as a defense against the hedge funds? By using it to buy local stocks—

thereby driving their prices up and causing the hedge funds, which had sold those stocks short, to lose money. Of course, in order to be effective these purchases would have to be on a large scale, comparable to or even greater than the hedge funds' short sales. But the authorities certainly had the resources to make such purchases.

Why, then, hadn't the hedge funds expected this response? Because they didn't think the Hong Kong government would be willing to risk the inevitable reaction from conservatives horrified that such a free-market paragon would try to manipulate market prices. And the reaction was fierce indeed. The government's actions were "insane," thundered Milton Friedman. The Heritage Foundation formally removed the city-state's designation as a bastion of economic freedom; newspaper stories linked Hong Kong with Malaysia, which had just imposed draconian capital controls. Finance Secretary Donald Tsang began touring the world, trying to explain the actions to investors and reassure them that his government was as pro-capitalism as ever. But it was an uphill fight.

For a time the hedge funds expected that the reaction would force the Hong Kong authorities to back down. They rolled over their short positions (i.e., paid the original owners of the stock additional fees for the right to put off their return) and settled in to wait the government out. The government then upped the ante, instituting new rules that restricted short-selling, thereby forcing the Hong Kong investors who had rented out their stocks to call them in; this forced the hedge funds to unwind their positions, but raised further howls of outrage.

And then the whole Hong Kong issue faded away, as a bizarre series of events around the world forced the hedge funds themselves to curtail their activities.

The Potemkin Economy

In 1787, the empress Catherine of Russia toured her empire's southern provinces. According to legend, her chief minister, Grigori Aleksandrovich Potemkin, stayed one day ahead, setting up false fronts that made wretched villages look prosperous, then dismantling the props and leapfrogging them to the next destination. Ever since, the term "Potemkin village" has been used to refer to apparently happy scenes that are in reality nothing but facades, bearing no relation to what really lies behind them.

It is entirely appropriate, then, that in the second half of the 1990s Russia itself became a sort of Potemkin economy.

Nobody found the transition from socialism to capitalism easy, but Russia found it harder than most. For years after the fall of Communism its economy seemed caught in a sort of limbo, having lost whatever guidance central planning used to provide, yet without having managed to achieve a working market system either. Even the things that used to work to some extent no longer functioned: factories that used to produce low-quality goods produced nothing at all, collective farms became even less productive than they were before, and the dreary Brezhnev years began to seem like a golden age. There were hundreds of thousands of highly skilled programmers, engineers, scientists, mathematicians, but they couldn't find decent work.

It was a sorry state of affairs, but Russia had one last asset: as the heir of the Soviet Union, it still had a massive arsenal of nuclear weapons. It didn't explicitly threaten to sell nukes to the highest bidder, but the risk that it might conditioned Western policy, making the U.S. government anxious to put the best face on things. Long after most informed people had become thoroughly cynical, the United States continued to hope that Russia's reformers would somehow manage to complete the stalled transition, that the oli-garchs would stop being so selfish or at least so shortsighted. So the U.S. government bullied the International Monetary Fund into lending money to Russia to buy time for stabilization plans that somehow never materialized. (*The Medley Report*, an international economic newsletter, commented that the United States was not, as some said, throwing money down a rathole. Instead, it was throwing money down a missile silo.)

The apparent ability of Russia to use its nuclear arms as col-lateral, in turn, encouraged high-rolling foreign investors to take a risk and put money into Russia. Everyone knew that the ruble might well be devalued, perhaps massively, or that the Russian gov-ernment might simply default on its debts. But it seemed a good bet that before that happened, the West would step in with yet another emergency cash injection. Since Russian government debt was offering extremely high interest rates, eventually reaching 150 percent, the bet was an appealing one to investors with a high tol-erance for risk—notably hedge funds.

However, it turned out that the bet wasn't that good after all. In the summer of 1998 Russia's financial situation unraveled faster than expected. In August, George Soros (!) suggested publicly that Russia devalue the ruble and then establish a currency board. His remarks triggered a run on the currency, an inadequate Mexican-style devaluation, and then a combination of currency collapse and debt moratorium. And the West had apparently had enough: there was no rescue this time. Suddenly claims on Russia could be sold, if at all, for a fraction of their face value, and billions of dollars had been lost. (What happened to that nuclear collateral? Good ques-tion; let's not think about it.)

In sheer dollar terms the money lost in Russia was quite trivial—no more than is lost when, for example, the U.S. stock market falls by a fraction of a percent, which it does almost every other day. But these losses fell heavily on a small group of highly leveraged financial operators, which meant that they had almost ridiculously large effects on the rest of the world. Indeed, for a few weeks it looked as if Russia's financial collapse would drag down the whole world.

The Panic of 1998

In the summer of 1998 the balance sheets of the world's hedge funds were not only huge but also immensely complex. Still, there was a pattern. Typically these funds were short in assets that were safe—not likely to plunge in value—and liquid—that is, easy to sell if you needed cash. At the same time, they were long in assets that were risky and illiquid. Thus a hedge fund might be short in German government debt, which is safe and easy to sell, and long in Danish mortgage-backed securities (indirect claims on houses), which are a bit more risky and a lot harder to sell at short notice. Or they might be short in Japanese bonds and long in Russian debt.

The general principle here was that historically markets have tended to place a rather high premium on both safety and liquidity, because small investors were risk-averse and never knew when they might need to cash out. This offered an opportunity to big operators, who could minimize the risk by careful diversification (buying a mix of assets so that gains on one would normally offset losses on another), and who would not normally find themselves suddenly in need of cash. It was largely by exploiting these margins that hedge funds made so much money, year after year.

By 1998, however, many people understood this basic idea, and competition among the hedge funds themselves had made it increasingly difficult to make money. Some hedge funds actually started returning investors' money, declaring that they could not find enough profitable opportunities to use it. But they also tried to find new opportunities by stretching even further, taking complex positions that appeared on the surface to be hugely risky but that supposedly were cunningly constructed to minimize the chance of losses.

What nobody realized until catastrophe struck was that the competition among hedge funds to exploit ever narrower profit opportunities had created a sort of financial doomsday machine.

Here's how it worked. Suppose that some hedge fund—call it Relativity Fund—has taken a big bet in Russian government debt. Then Russia defaults, and it loses a billion dollars or so. This makes the investors who are the counterparts of Relativity's short positions—the people who have lent it stocks and bonds, to be returned in the future—nervous. So they demand their assets back. However, Relativity doesn't actually have those assets on hand; it must buy them back, which means that it must sell other assets to get the necessary cash. And since it is such a big player in the markets, when it starts selling, the prices of the things it has invested in go down.

Meanwhile, Relativity's rival, the Pussycat Fund, has also invested in many of the same things. So when Relativity is forced into sudden large sales, this means big losses for Pussycat as well; it too finds itself forced to "cover its shorts" by selling, driving the prices of other assets down. In so doing, it creates a problem for the Elizabethan Fund, and so on down the line.

If all this reminds you of the story of Asia's financial meltdown, as I told it in Chapter 4, it should: at a fundamental level it was the same kind of process, involving plunging prices and imploding balance sheets—a vicious cycle of deleveraging. Nobody thought that such a thing could happen in the modern world, but it did, and the consequences were startling.

You see, it turned out that the hedge funds had been so assiduous about arbitraging away liquidity and risk premia that for many illiquid assets they *were* the market; when they all tried to sell at once, there were no alternative buyers. And so after years of steadily narrowing, liquidity and risk premia suddenly surged to unheard-of levels as hedge funds were forced to unwind their positions. Twenty-nine-year U.S. government bonds—a perfectly safe asset, in the sense that if the U.S. government goes, so does everything else—were offering significantly higher interest rates than thirty-year bonds, which are traded in a larger market and are therefore slightly easier to sell. Corporate bonds normally offer higher returns than U.S. government debt, but the spread had suddenly widened by several percentage points. And commercial mortgage-backed securities—the financial instruments that indirectly fund most nonresidential real estate construction—could not be sold at all. At one meeting I attended, participants asked a Federal Reserve official who had described the situation what could be done to resolve it. "Pray," he replied.

In fact, luckily, the Fed did more than that. First of all, it engineered the rescue of the most famous casualty among the hedge funds: Connecticut-based Long Term Capital Management.

The saga of LTCM is even more remarkable than the legend of George Soros. Soros is a figure in a long tradition, that of the swashbuckling financial raider—not that different, when you get to essentials, from Jim Fisk or Jay Gould. The managers at Long Term Capital, however, were quintessentially modern types: nerd savants using formulas and computers to outsmart the market. The firm boasted two Nobel laureates, and many of their best students, on its payroll. They believed that by carefully studying the historical correlations between assets, they could construct clever portfolios—long in some assets, short in others—that yielded high returns with much less risk than people imagined. And year after year they delivered, with such regularity that, it turned out, people who lent them money stopped even asking whether the firm really had enough capital to be a safe partner.

Then the markets went crazy.

It is still unclear whether the losses that LTCM suffered were the result of once-in-a-lifetime shocks that could not have been anticipated, or whether the computer models they used were naive in not allowing for the occasional large market disturbance. (And also whether this naïveté, if that was what it was, was deliberate— moral hazard again.) Whatever the cause, by September the company was facing margin calls—demands that it either put more cash on deposit with the lenders or pay up in full—that it could not meet. And suddenly it became clear that LTCM had become so large a player in the markets that if it failed, and its positions were liquidated, it might precipitate a full-scale panic.

Something had to be done. In the end, no public money was required: the New York Fed was able to persuade a group of investors to take over majority ownership of LTCM in return for a desperately needed injection of cash. As it turned out, once markets had calmed down again, the banks actually made a profit on the deal.

Even with the rescue, however, it was by no means a foregone conclusion that the crisis would be surmounted. When the Federal Reserve cut interest rates by only 0.25 percent at its regularly scheduled September meeting, the size of the cut disappointed the markets, and the already troubled financial situation started to look like a runaway panic. Suddenly people were starting to draw analogies between the financial crisis and the bank runs that plunged the United States into the Great Depression; J.P. Morgan even went so far as to flatly predict a severe recession in 1999.

But the Fed had a trick up its sleeve. Normally interest rate changes take place only when the Federal Open Market Committee meets, roughly every six weeks. In that September meeting, however, the committee had granted Alan Greenspan the discretionary power to cut interest rates a further quarter point whenever necessary. On October 15 he surprised the markets by announcing that cut—and, miraculously, the markets rallied. When the Fed cut rates yet again at its next meeting, the panic turned into euphoria. By the end of 1998 all the unusual liquidity premia had vanished, and the stock market was once again setting new records.

It is important to realize that even now Fed officials are not quite sure how they pulled this rescue off. At the height of the crisis it seemed entirely possible that cutting interest rates would be entirely ineffectual—after all, if nobody can borrow, what difference does it make what the price would be if they could? And if everyone had believed that the world was coming to an end, their panic might—as in so many other countries—have ended up being a self-fulfilling prophecy. In retrospect Greenspan seemed to have been like a general who rides out in front of his demoralized army, waves his sword and shouts encouragement, and somehow turns the tide of battle: well done, but not something you would want to count on working next time.

Indeed, some Fed officials fretted that the public was overrating their abilities—a new form of moral hazard, said one Greenspan adviser, based on the belief that the Fed could bail the economy and the markets out of any crisis. Sure enough, the limits of the Fed's power were graphically demonstrated when the crisis of 2008 hit.

Before we get to that, however, let's talk about the legend of Alan Greenspan, and how it all went wrong.

7

GREENSPAN'S BUBBLES

For more than eighteen years, from May 1987 to January 2006, Alan Greenspan was the chairman of the Federal Reserve's Board of Governors. The position, in itself, made him one of the world's most powerful financial officials. But Greenspan's influence went far beyond his formal powers: he was the Maestro, the Oracle, the senior member of the Committee to Save the World, as a 1999 cover story in *Time* put it.

When Greenspan left office, he did so trailing clouds of glory. Alan Blinder of Princeton University pronounced him possibly the greatest central banker in history. When Greenspan made one of his final appearances before Congress, he was hailed virtually as a monetary messiah: "You have guided monetary policy through stock-market crashes, wars, terrorist attacks and natural disasters," declared one congressman. "You have made a great contribution to the prosperity of the U.S. and the nation is in your debt."

Almost three years later, Greenspan's name was mud.

The story of the rise and fall of Alan Greenspan's reputation is more than a personal morality tale. It's also the story of how the makers of economic policy convinced themselves that they had everything under control, only to learn, to their horror—and the country's pain—that they didn't.

The Age of Greenspan

How did Greenspan become such a legend? In large part because he presided over a period of generally good economic news. The 1970s and early 1980s were an era of nasty shocks—of inflation and unemployment rates that went into double digits, of the worst economic slumps since the Great Depression. By contrast, the Greenspan era was relatively serene. Inflation stayed low through- out, and the two recessions during his tenure were brief, eight- month affairs, at least according to the official chronology (more on that later). Jobs were relatively plentiful: in the late 1990s and again in the middle of the next decade, the unemployment rate fell to levels not seen since the 1960s. And for financial investors, the Greenspan years were heavenly: the Dow soared past 10,000, and stock prices on average rose more than 10 percent a year.

How much credit did Greenspan deserve for this good perfor- mance? Less than he received, surely. It was Greenspan's predeces- sor, Paul Volcker, who brought inflation under control, achieving that goal with tight-money policies that caused a severe economic slump but finally broke the back of inflationary psychology. After Volcker did the hard, unpopular work, Greenspan was able to bask in the payoff.

Much of the good economic news also had little to do with

monetary policy. During the Greenspan years American businesses finally figured out how to use information technology effectively. When a new technology is introduced, it often takes a while before the economic benefits become apparent, because it takes time for businesses to rearrange their structure to take proper advantage of the innovation. The classic example is electricity. Although electrical machinery became widely available in the 1880s, at first businesses continued to build factories the old way: multistory buildings with machines crammed into narrow spaces, a design dictated by the need to have a big steam engine in the basement run all the shafts and pulleys. It wasn't until after World War I that businesses began taking advantage of the fact that they no longer needed a central power source, by switching to one-story, open-plan factories with plenty of room to move materials around.

The same thing happened with information technology. The microprocessor was invented in 1971, and personal computers were widespread by the early 1980s. But for a long time offices continued to be run the way they had been in the age of carbon paper. It wasn't until the mid-1990s that businesses really began taking advantage of the new technology to create networked offices, continuous-time updates of inventory, and so on. When they did, there was a sharp acceleration in the growth rate of U.S. productivity—the amount an average worker produces in an hour. This lifted profits and helped control inflation, contributing to the good economic news under Greenspan; but the Fed chairman had nothing to do with it.

Although Greenspan didn't beat inflation or create the productivity revolution, he did have a distinctive approach to monetary management that seemed to work well at the time. The operative word here may be "seemed," but before we get to that, let's look at what was distinctive about Greenspan's reign as chairman.

America's Designated Driver

Alan Greenspan wasn't the longest-serving Fed chairman ever. That honor went to William McChesney Martin Jr., who ran the Fed from 1951 to 1970. The two men's monetary philosophies couldn't have been more different.

Martin famously declared that the Fed's job was "to take away the punch bowl just as the party gets going." By that he mainly meant that the Fed should raise interest rates to prevent a booming economy from overheating, which could cause inflation. But his remark was also interpreted to mean that the Fed should try to prevent "irrational exuberance"—Greenspan's phrase—in the financial markets.

While Greenspan warned against excessive exuberance, however, he never *did* much about it. He used the phrase "irrational exuberance" in a 1996 speech in which he suggested, without quite saying it, that there was a bubble in stock prices. But he didn't raise interest rates to curb the market's enthusiasm; he didn't even seek to impose margin requirements on stock market investors. Instead, he waited until the bubble burst, as it did in 2000, then tried to clean up the mess afterward.

As an article in Reuters caustically but accurately put it, Greenspan acted like a parent who sternly warns teenagers against overdoing it but doesn't actually stop the party, and stands ready to act as designated driver when the fun is over.

To be fair to Greenspan, many economists, from both sides of the political spectrum, agreed with this policy doctrine. And the truth is that Greenspan's willingness to let the good times roll served the

U.S. economy well in at least one respect: the spectacular job creation during the Clinton years probably wouldn't have been quite
as spectacular if someone else had been in charge at the Fed.

The figure below, which shows the U.S. unemployment rate since
the beginning of 1987, tells the tale.* Official recession dates are
indicated by the shaded bars. The dominating feature of this graph
is the extraordinary decline in unemployment from 1993 to 2000,
a decline that brought the unemployment rate below 4 percent
for the first time since 1970. Now, Greenspan didn't cause this
decline, but he did let it happen. And his benign neglect toward
the unemployment decline was both unorthodox and, it turned
out, the right thing to do.

In the early to mid-1990s the conventional view (which I shared
myself) was that inflation would start accelerating if the unemployment rate fell below about 5.5 percent. That seemed to be

* Source: 2008 Federal Reserve Bank of St. Louis. Civilian unemployment rate
from U.S. Department of Labor's Bureau of Labor Statistics; data on U.S. recessions
from NBER.

the lesson of the previous couple of decades. In fact, inflation had accelerated right on cue in the late 1980s when the unemployment rate closed in on 5 percent. When the unemployment rate fell through the traditional red line in the mid-1990s, a chorus of economists urged Greenspan to raise interest rates to prevent a resurgence of inflation.

Greenspan, however, refused to fire before he saw the whites of inflation's eyes. He speculated publicly that the acceleration of productivity growth might have changed the historic relationship between low unemployment and accelerating inflation, and used this argument to put off any interest rate increase until there was clear evidence that inflation actually was on the rise. And it turned out that something had, in fact, changed in the economy. (Economists are still arguing about what.) Unemployment fell to levels not seen in decades, yet inflation remained quiescent. And the nation felt a sense of prosperity it hadn't experienced since the sixties.

When it came to job creation, then, letting the punch bowl stay out while the party went on turned out to be an excellent move. When it came to irrational exuberance in the asset markets, however, Greenspanism was less successful. Only after Greenspan had left office would it become clear just *how* unsuccessful he had been.

Greenspan's Bubbles

As I've just noted, Greenspan warned about irrational exuberance, but he didn't do anything about it. And in fact, the Fed chairman holds what I believe is a unique record among central bankers: he presided over not one but two enormous asset bubbles, first in stocks, then in housing.

The graph on this page shows the timing and size of these two bubbles. One line shows the ratio of stock prices to corporate earnings, a commonly used indicator of whether stocks are reasonably priced. The other shows a comparable measure for housing prices, the ratio of average U.S. home prices to average rents, expressed as an index, with 1987 equaling 100. You can clearly see the stock bubble of the 1990s, followed by the housing bubble of the next decade.* Overall, housing prices never got quite as far out of line with historical norms as stock prices did. But that's misleading, in several respects. First, housing is a bigger deal than the stock market, especially for middle-class families, whose houses are usually their main asset. Second, the boom in housing prices was uneven:

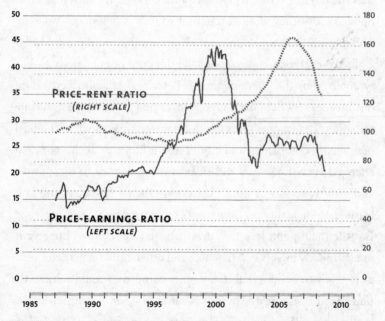

* The price-earnings ratio in the figure is from Robert Shiller of Yale University, who compares stock prices with average earnings over the previous decade—to smooth out short-run fluctuations in profits due to booms and slumps. The house price index is the Case-Shiller national index, while rents are taken from the Bureau of Economic Analysis.

in the central part of the United States, where land is abundant, housing prices never rose much more than overall inflation, but in coastal areas, especially Florida and southern California, prices soared to well over twice their normal ratio to rents. Finally, the financial system turned out to be much more vulnerable to the side effects of falling home prices than it was to the side effects of a stock bust, for reasons that I'll explain in Chapter 9.

How did these bubbles happen?

The stock bubble of the 1990s probably mainly reflected two things. One of them, extreme optimism about the profit potential of information technology, has received a lot of attention. The other, the growing sense of security about the economy, the belief that the days of severe recessions were over, hasn't gotten as much publicity. But they worked together to push stock prices to astonishing levels.

Today, everyone knows about the dot-com bubble, perhaps best symbolized by the phenomenon of Pets.com, which turned a dubious business model plus a clever ad campaign into an astonishing valuation. But it wasn't just the dot-coms. Across much of the business sector, companies told stories about how new technology had changed everything, how old rules about the limits to their profits and growth no longer applied. In more than a few cases, we later learned, these feel-good stories were buttressed by accounting fraud. But the main point was that investors, having seen the huge gains made by early buyers of Microsoft and other entrants in the IT field, were ready to believe that many other companies could achieve the same kind of miracle. There was, of course, an adding-up fallacy in all of this: there wasn't room in the economy for all the future Microsofts people thought they saw. But hype springs eternal, and people were willing to suspend their rational faculties.

There also seemed to be more serious reasons to buy stocks.

It was well known among economists and financial experts that stocks had, historically, been very good investments, at least for people who were willing to buy and hold. There was even an extensive literature in economics about the puzzle of the "equity premium": stocks consistently did so much better than alternative investments like bonds that it was hard to understand why people didn't put all their money into equities. The answer, probably, was fear: the big stock losses of the 1930s, and the more recent memory of how stocks swooned in the face of stagflation during the 1970s—the real value of stocks fell about 7 percent a year between 1968 and 1978—kept investors cautious. But as the Great Moderation persisted, with inflation low and no severe recessions, the fear gradually ebbed. Books like *Dow 36,000*, which was based on a garbled version of the equity premium literature (the authors did the calculation all wrong, but hey, who was counting?), became best-sellers.

And as stock prices rose, they began to feed on themselves. Never mind the more or less reasonable arguments in favor of stock investing; by 1998 or so, what people saw was that anyone who bought stocks had made lots of money, while anyone who waited on the sidelines was being left behind. So more and more funds poured into the stock market, prices rose ever higher, and the bubble expanded, seemingly without limit.

But there was, of course, a limit. As Robert Shiller, the author of *Irrational Exuberance*, has pointed out, an asset bubble is a sort of natural Ponzi scheme in which people keep making money as long as there are more suckers to draw in. But eventually the scheme runs out of suckers, and the whole thing crashes. In the case of stocks, the peak came in the summer of 2000. Over the next two years, stocks lost on average about 40 percent of their value.

The next bubble began inflating shortly thereafter.

The housing bubble was, in some sense, even less justified than the stock bubble of the previous decade. Yes, it was foolish to get so excited over Pets.com and all that, but the truth was that there was an exciting new technological universe opening up for exploitation. Add to that the fact that macroeconomic performance really had improved—stagflation had receded as a threat, and the business cycle seemed to have moderated—and there was a case for believing that some old rules no longer applied.

But what justified a bubble in housing? We know why home prices started rising: interest rates were very low in the early years of this decade, for reasons I'll explain shortly, which made buying houses attractive. And there's no question that this justified some rise in prices.

It did not, however, justify the belief that all the old rules no longer applied. Houses are houses; Americans have long been in the habit of buying houses with borrowed money, but it's hard to see why anyone should have believed, circa 2003, that the basic principles of such borrowing had been repealed. From long experience, we knew that home buyers shouldn't take on mortgages whose payments they couldn't afford, and that they should put enough money down so that they can sustain a moderate drop in home prices and still have positive equity. Low interest rates should have changed the mortgage payments associated with a given amount of borrowing, but not much else.

What actually happened, however, was a complete abandonment of traditional principles. To some extent this was driven by the irrational exuberance of individual families who saw house prices rising ever higher and decided that they should jump into the market, and not worry about how to make the payments. But it was driven to a greater extent by a change in lending practices. Buyers were given loans requiring little or no down payment, and with monthly bills that were well beyond their ability to afford—or at least would be unaffordable once the initial low, teaser interest rate reset. Much though not all of this dubious lending went under the heading of "subprime," but the phenomenon was much broader than that. And it wasn't just low-income or minority home buyers who were taking on more than they could handle; it was happening across the board.

Why did lenders relax their standards? First, they came to believe in ever-rising home prices. As long as home prices only go up, it doesn't matter much from the lender's point of view whether a borrower can make his or her payments: if the payments are too high, well, the buyer can either take out a home equity loan to get more cash or, if worst comes to worst, just sell the home and pay off the mortgage. Second, the lenders didn't concern themselves with the quality of their loans because they didn't hold on to them. Instead, they sold them to investors, who didn't understand what they were buying.

"Securitization" of home mortgages—assembling large pools of mortgages, then selling investors shares in the payments received from borrowers—isn't a new practice. In fact, it was pioneered by Fannie Mae, the government-sponsored lending agency, which dates back to the 1930s. Until the great housing bubble, however, securitization was more or less completely limited to "prime" mortgages: loans to borrowers who could make a substantial down payment and had enough income to meet the mortgage payments. Such borrowers still defaulted now and then, in the wake of job loss or medical emergency, but default rates were low, and buyers of mortgage-backed securities more or less knew what they were buying.

The financial innovation that made securitization of subprime mortgages possible was the collateralized debt obligation, or CDO.

A CDO offered shares in the payments from a mortgage pool—
but not all shares were created equal. Instead, some shares were
"senior," receiving first claim on the payments from the mortgagees. Only once those claims were satisfied was money sent to less
senior shares. In principle, this was supposed to make the senior
shares a very safe investment: even if some mortgagees defaulted,
how likely was it that enough would default to pose problems
for the cash flow to these senior shares? (Quite likely, it turned
out—but that wasn't understood at the time.) And so the rating
agencies were willing to classify senior shares in CDOs as AAA,
even if the underlying mortgages were highly dubious. This opened
up large-scale financing of subprime lending, because there are
many institutional investors, such as pension funds, that won't
buy anything except AAA securities but were quite willing to buy
AAA-rated assets that yielded significantly higher returns than
ordinary bonds.

As long as housing prices kept rising, everything looked fine and
the Ponzi scheme kept rolling. There were few defaults, mortgage-
backed securities yielded high returns, and funds continued to
pour into the housing market. Some economists, including yours
truly, warned that there was a major housing bubble, and that its
bursting would pose serious risks to the economy. But authoritative
figures declared otherwise. Alan Greenspan, in particular, declared
that any major decline in home prices would be "most unlikely."
There might, he conceded, be some "froth" in local housing markets, but there wasn't a national bubble.

But there was, and it began deflating in 2006—slowly at first,
then with increasing speed. By that time Greenspan was no longer
chairman of the Fed, having been succeeded by Ben Bernanke.
But Greenspanism still held sway: the Fed (and the Bush administration) believed that the effects of the housing bust could be "con-

tained," that Bernanke, like Greenspan, could serve as America's designated driver.

Yet the experience after the stock bubble popped should have been a clear warning that this confidence was misplaced.

When Bubbles Burst

The story of the aftermath of the 1990s stock bubble is usually told this way: After the bubble burst, the U.S. economy fell into recession. But Greenspan aggressively cut interest rates and quickly turned the situation around. The recession was shallow, with no big declines in GDP, and short, ending after only eight months.

The real story is this: Officially the recession was short, but the job market kept deteriorating long after the recession had officially been declared over. You can see this in the figure on p. 143: the unemployment rate rose steeply during the recession (the shaded bar) but continued to rise in the months that followed. The period of deteriorating employment actually lasted two and a half years, not eight months.

You might ask why, in this case, the recession was declared over so soon. Well, in the United States the official starting and ending dates of recessions are determined by an independent committee of economists associated with the National Bureau of Economic Research. The committee looks at a variety of indicators— employment, industrial production, consumer spending, GDP. If all these indicators are going down, a recession is declared. If several of them turn up again, the recession is declared over. By late 2001, industrial production and GDP were rising, though slowly, so that indicated the end of the official recession. But as we've seen, the job market was still getting worse.

And the Fed was deeply worried about the weakness of the job market and the general sluggishness of the economy, which seemed all too reminiscent of Japan in the 1990s. Greenspan would later write that he was concerned about the possibility of "corrosive deflation." So he kept cutting rates, eventually bringing the Federal funds rate down to just 1 percent.

When monetary policy finally did get traction, it was through the housing market. Cynics said that Greenspan had succeeded only by replacing the stock bubble with a housing bubble—and they were right. And the question everyone should have been asking (but few were) was, What will happen when the housing bubble bursts? The Fed was barely able to pull the economy out of its post-stock-bubble slump, and even then it was able to do so only because it was lucky enough to have another bubble come along at the right time. Would the Fed be able to pull off the feat again?

In the event, the consequences when the housing bubble burst were worse than almost anyone imagined. Why? Because the financial system had changed in ways that nobody fully appreciated.

8

BANKING IN THE SHADOWS

B anks are wonderful things, when they work. And they usually do. But when they don't, all hell can break loose—as it has in the United States and much of the world over the course of the past year.

But wasn't the age of banking crises supposed to have ended seventy years ago? Aren't banks regulated, insured, guaranteed up the wazoo? Yes and no. Yes for traditional banks; no for a large part of the modern, de facto banking system.

To understand the problem, it helps to run through a brief, selective history of banking and bank regulation.

The History of Banking, Simplified

Modern banks are supposed to have originated with goldsmiths, whose primary business was making jewelry but who developed a profitable sideline as keepers of other people's coin: since gold-smiths' shops had good safes, they provided more secure places for the wealthy to stash their cash than, say, a strongbox under the bed. (Think of Silas Marner.)

At some point goldsmiths discovered that they could make their sideline as keepers of coin even more profitable by taking some of the coin deposited in their care and lending it out at interest. You might think this would get them in trouble: what if the own-ers of the coin showed up and demanded it right away? But what the goldsmiths realized was that the law of averages made this unlikely: on any given day some of their depositors would show up and demand their coin back, but most would not. So it was enough to keep a fraction of the coin in reserve; the rest could be put to work. And thus banking was born.

Every once in a while, however, things would go spectacularly wrong. There would be a rumor—maybe true, maybe false—that a bank's investments had gone bad, that it no longer had enough assets to repay its depositors. The rumor would cause a rush by depositors to get their money out before it was all gone—what we call "a run on the bank." And often such a run would break the bank even if the original rumor was false: in order to raise cash quickly, the bank would have to sell off assets at fire-sale prices, and sure enough, at those prices it *wouldn't* have enough assets to pay what it owed. Since runs based even on false rumors could break healthy institutions, bank runs became self-fulfilling prophe-cies: a bank might collapse, not because there was a rumor about its investments having gone bad, but simply because there was a rumor that it was about to suffer from a run.

And one thing that could cause such a rumor is the fact that other banks had already suffered from bank runs. The history of the U.S. financial system before the Great Depression is punctuated by "panics": the Panic of 1873, the Panic of 1907, and so on. These panics were, for the most part, series of contagious bank runs in which each bank's collapse undermined confidence in other banks, and financial institutions fell like a row of dominoes.

By the way, any resemblance between this description of pre-Depression panics and the financial contagion that swept Asia in the late 1990s is not at all coincidental. All financial crises tend to bear a family resemblance to one another.

The problem of banking panics led to a search for solutions. Between the Civil War and World War I the United States did not have a central bank—the Federal Reserve was created in 1913—but it did have a system of "national banks" that were subject to a modest degree of regulation. Also, in some locations bankers pooled their resources to create local clearinghouses that would jointly guarantee a member's liabilities in the event of a panic, and some state governments began offering deposit insurance on their banks' deposits.

The Panic of 1907, however, showed the limitations of this system (and eerily prefigured our current crisis). The crisis originated in institutions in New York known as "trusts," bank-like institutions that accepted deposits but were originally intended to manage only inheritances and estates for wealthy clients. Because they were supposed to engage only in low-risk activities, trusts were less regulated and had lower reserve requirements and lower cash reserves than national banks. However, as the economy boomed during the first decade of the twentieth century, trusts began speculating in real estate and the stock market, areas from which national banks were prohibited. Because they were less regulated than national banks, trusts were able to pay their depositors higher returns. Meanwhile, trusts took a free ride on national banks' reputation for soundness, with depositors considering them equally safe. As a result, trusts grew rapidly: by 1907, the total value of the assets in the trusts in New York City was as high as the total in the national banks. Meanwhile, the trusts declined to join the New York Clearinghouse, a consortium of New York City national banks that guaranteed each other's soundness, because that would have required the trusts to hold higher cash reserves, reducing their profits.

The Panic of 1907 began with the demise of the Knickerbocker Trust, a large New York City trust that failed when it financed an unsuccessful large-scale speculation in the stock market. Quickly, other New York trusts came under pressure, with frightened depositors queuing in long lines to withdraw their funds. The New York Clearinghouse declined to step in and lend to the trusts, and even healthy ones came under serious assault. Within two days a dozen major trusts had gone under. Credit markets froze, and the stock market fell dramatically as stock traders were unable to get credit to finance their trades and business confidence evaporated.

Fortunately, New York City's wealthiest man, a banker by the name of J. P. Morgan, quickly stepped in to stop the panic. Understanding that the crisis was spreading and would soon engulf healthy institutions, trusts and banks alike, he worked with other bankers, wealthy men such as John D. Rockefeller, and the U.S. secretary of the treasury to shore up the reserves of banks and trusts so they could withstand the onslaught of withdrawals. Once people were assured that they could withdraw their money, the panic ceased. While the panic itself lasted little more than a week, it and the stock market collapse decimated the economy. A four-year recession ensued, with production falling 11 percent and unemployment rising from 3 to 8 percent.

Although disaster had been narrowly avoided, counting on J. P. Morgan to save the world a second time didn't seem like a good idea, even in the Gilded Age. So the Panic of 1907 was followed by banking reform. In 1913 the national banking system was eliminated, and the Federal Reserve System was created with the goal of compelling all deposit-taking institutions to hold adequate reserves and open their accounts to inspection by regulators. Although the new regime standardized and centralized the holding of bank reserves, it didn't eliminate the threat of bank runs—and the most severe banking crisis in history emerged in the early 1930s. As the economy slumped, commodity prices plunged; this hit highly indebted American farmers hard, precipitating a series of loan defaults followed by bank runs in 1930, 1931, and 1933, each of which started at Midwestern banks and then spread throughout the country. There's more or less unanimous agreement among economic historians that the banking crisis is what turned a nasty recession into the Great Depression.

The response was the creation of a system with many more safeguards. The Glass-Steagall Act separated banks into two kinds: commercial banks, which accepted deposits, and investment banks, which didn't. Commercial banks were sharply restricted in the risks they could take; in return, they had ready access to credit from the Fed (the so-called discount window), and, probably most important of all, their deposits were insured by the taxpayer. Investment banks were much less tightly regulated, but that was considered acceptable because as nondepository institutions they weren't supposed to be subject to bank runs.

This new system protected the economy from financial crises for almost seventy years. Things often went wrong—most notably, in the 1980s a combination of bad luck and bad policy led to the failure of many savings and loans, a special kind of bank that had become the dominant source of housing loans. Since S&L deposits were federally insured, taxpayers ended up footing the bill, which ended up being about 5 percent of GDP (the equivalent of more than $700 billion now). The fall of the S&Ls led to a temporary credit crunch, which was one major cause of the 1990–91 recession, visible in the figure on p. 143. But that was as bad as it got. The age of banking crises, we were told, was over.

It wasn't.

The Shadow Banking System

What is a bank?

That can sound like a stupid question. We all know what a bank looks like: it's a big marble building—okay, these days it might also be a storefront in a shopping mall—with tellers accepting and handing out cash, and an "FDIC insured" sign in the window.

But from an economist's point of view, banks are defined not by what they look like but by what they do. From the days of those enterprising goldsmiths to the present day, the essential feature of banking is the way it promises ready access to cash for those who place money in its care, even while investing most of that money in assets that can't be liquidated on a moment's notice. Any institution or arrangement that does this is a bank, whether or not it lives in a big marble building.

Consider, for example, an arrangement known as an auction-rate security, which was invented at Lehman Brothers in 1984 and became a preferred source of funding for many institutions, ranging from the Port Authority of New York and New Jersey to New York's Metropolitan Museum of Art. The arrangement worked like this: Individuals would lend money to the borrowing institution on a long-term basis; legally, the money might be tied up for thirty

years. At frequent intervals, however, often once a week, the institution would hold a small auction in which potential new investors
would bid for the right to replace investors who wanted to get out.
The interest rate determined by this bidding process would apply
to all funds invested in the security until the next auction was held,
and so on. If the auction failed—if there weren't enough bidders
to let everyone who wanted out to leave—the interest rate would
rise to a penalty rate, say 15 percent; but that wasn't expected to
happen. The idea of an auction-rate security was that it would rec-
oncile the desire of borrowers for secure long-term funding with
the desire of lenders for ready access to their money.

But that's exactly what a bank does.

Yet auction-rate securities seemed to offer everyone a better
deal than conventional banking. Investors in auction-rate securities
were paid higher interest rates than they would have received on
bank deposits, while the issuers of these securities paid lower rates
than they would have on long-term bank loans. There's no such
thing as a free lunch, Milton Friedman told us, yet auction-rate
securities seemed to offer just that. How did they do that?

Well, the answer seems obvious, at least in retrospect: Banks
are highly regulated; they are required to hold liquid reserves,
maintain substantial capital, and pay into the deposit insurance
system. By raising funds via auction-rate securities, borrowers
could bypass these regulations and their attendant expense. But
that also meant that auction-rate securities weren't protected by
the banking safety net.

And sure enough, the auction-rate security system, which contained $400 billion at its peak, collapsed in early 2008. One after
another, auctions failed, as too few new investors arrived to let existing investors get their money out. People who thought they had

ready access to their cash suddenly discovered that their money was, instead, tied up in decades-long investments they couldn't get out of. And each auction failure led to another: having seen the perils of these too-clever investment schemes, who wanted to put fresh money into the system?

What happened to auction-rate securities was, in all but name, a contagious series of bank runs.

The parallel to the Panic of 1907 should be obvious. In the early years of the twentieth century, the trusts, the bank-like institutions that seemed to offer a better deal because they were able to operate outside the regulatory system, grew rapidly, only to become the epicenter of a financial crisis. A century later, the same thing happened.

Today, the set of institutions and arrangements that act as "nonbank banks" are generally referred to either as the "parallel banking system" or as the "shadow banking system." I think the latter term is more descriptive as well as more picturesque. Conventional banks, which take deposits and are part of the Federal Reserve system, operate more or less in the sunlight, with open books and regulators looking over their shoulders. The operations of nondepository institutions that are de facto banks, by contrast, are far more obscure. Indeed, until the crisis hit, few people seem to have appreciated just how important the shadow banking system had become.

In June 2008 Timothy Geithner, the president of the New York Federal Reserve Bank, gave a speech at the Economic Club of New York in which he tried to explain how the end of the housing bubble could have done as much financial damage as it did. (Geithner didn't know this, but the worst was yet to come.) Even though the speech was, necessarily, written in centralbankerese, with a hefty dose of jargon, Geithner's shock at how out of control the system had gotten comes through:

The structure of the financial system changed fundamentally during the boom, with dramatic growth in the share of assets outside the traditional banking system. This non-bank financial system grew to be very large, particularly in money and funding markets. In early 2007, asset-backed commercial paper conduits, in structured investment vehicles, in auction-rate preferred securities, tender option bonds and variable rate demand notes, had a combined asset size of roughly $2.2 trillion. Assets financed overnight in triparty repo grew to $2.5 trillion. Assets held in hedge funds grew to roughly $1.8 trillion. The combined balance sheets of the then five major investment banks totaled $4 trillion.

In comparison, the total assets of the top five bank holding companies in the United States at that point were just over $6 trillion, and total assets of the entire banking system were about $10 trillion.

Geithner, then, considered a whole range of financial arrangements, not just auction-rate securities, to be part of the "non-bank financial system": things that weren't banks from a regulatory point of view but were nonetheless performing banking functions. And he went on to point out just how vulnerable the new system was:

> The scale of long-term risky and relatively illiquid assets financed by very short-term liabilities made many of the vehicles and institutions in this parallel financial system vulnerable to a classic type of run, but without the protections such as deposit insurance that the banking system has in place to reduce such risks.

Indeed, several of the sectors he described have already collapsed: auction-rate securities have vanished, as already described;

asset-backed commercial paper (short-term debt issued by funds that invested the money in long-term assets, including mortgage-backed securities) has withered; two of the five major investment banks have failed and another has merged with a conventional bank; and so on. And it turns out that Geithner was missing some additional major points of vulnerability: the government in effect had to nationalize AIG, the world's largest insurance company, and the carry trade—an international financial arrangement that transferred funds from Japan and other low-interest-rate nations to higher-yielding investments elsewhere in the world—imploded as this new edition was going to press.

But let's postpone discussion of the crisis until the next chapter, and instead ask about the buildup to the crisis: why was the system allowed to become so vulnerable?

Malign Neglect

The financial crisis has, inevitably, led to a hunt for villains.

Some of the accusations are entirely spurious, like the claim, popular on the right, that all our problems were caused by the Community Reinvestment Act, which supposedly forced banks to lend to minority home buyers who then defaulted on their mortgages; in fact, the act was passed in 1977, which makes it hard to see how it can be blamed for a crisis that didn't happen until three decades later. Anyway, the act applied only to depository banks, which accounted for a small fraction of the bad loans during the housing bubble.

Other accusations have a grain of truth, but are more wrong than right. Conservatives like to blame Fannie Mae and Freddie Mac, the government-sponsored lenders that pioneered securitization, for the housing bubble and the fragility of the financial system. The grain of truth here is that Fannie and Freddie, which had grown enormously between 1990 and 2003—largely because they were filling the hole left by the collapse of many savings and loans—did make some imprudent loans, and suffered from accounting scandals besides. But the very scrutiny Fannie and Freddie attracted as a result of those scandals kept them mainly out of the picture during the housing bubble's most feverish period, from 2004 to 2006. As a result, the agencies played only a minor role in the epidemic of bad lending.

On the left, it's popular to blame deregulation for the crisis—specifically, the 1999 repeal of the Glass-Steagall Act, which allowed commercial banks to get into the investment banking business and thereby take on more risks. In retrospect, this was surely a move in the wrong direction, and it may have contributed in subtle ways to the crisis—for example, some of the risky financial structures created during the boom years were the "off balance sheet" operations of commercial banks. Yet the crisis, for the most part, hasn't involved problems with deregulated institutions that took new risks. Instead, it has involved risks taken by institutions that were never regulated in the first place.

And that, I'd argue, is the core of what happened. As the shadow banking system expanded to rival or even surpass conventional banking in importance, politicians and government officials should have realized that we were re-creating the kind of financial vulnerability that made the Great Depression possible—and they should have responded by extending regulation and the financial safety net to cover these new institutions. Influential figures should have proclaimed a simple rule: anything that does what a bank does, anything that has to be rescued in crises the way banks are, should be regulated like a bank.

In fact, the Long Term Capital Management crisis, described in

Chapter 6, should have served as an object lesson of the dangers posed by the shadow banking system. Certainly many people were aware of just how close the system had come to collapse.

But this warning was ignored, and there was no move to extend regulation. On the contrary, the spirit of the times—and the ideology of the George W. Bush administration—was deeply antiregulation. This attitude was symbolized by a photo-op held in 2003, in which representatives of the various agencies that play roles in bank oversight used pruning shears and a chainsaw to cut up stacks of regulations. More concretely, the Bush administration used federal power, including obscure powers of the Office of the Comptroller of the Currency, to block state-level efforts to impose some oversight on subprime lending.

Meanwhile, the people who should have been worrying about the fragility of the system were, instead, singing the praises of "financial innovation." "Not only have individual financial institutions become less vulnerable to shocks from underlying risk factors," declared Alan Greenspan in 2004, "but also the financial system as a whole has become more resilient."

So the growing risks of a crisis for the financial system and the economy as a whole were ignored or dismissed. And the crisis came.

9

THE SUM OF ALL FEARS

On July 19, 2007, the Dow Jones Industrial Average rose above 14,000 for the first time. Two weeks later the White House released a "fact sheet" boasting about the economy's performance on the Bush administration's watch: "The President's Pro-Growth Policies Are Helping Keep Our Economy Strong, Flexible, and Dynamic," it declared. What about the problems already visible in the housing market and in subprime mortgages? They were "largely contained," said Treasury Secretary Henry Paulson in an August 1 speech in Beijing.

On August 9 the French bank BNP Paribas suspended withdrawals from three of its funds—and the first great financial crisis of the twenty-first century had begun.

I'm tempted to say that the crisis is like nothing we've ever seen before. But it might be more accurate to say that it's like everything we've seen before, all at once: a bursting real estate bubble comparable to what happened in Japan at the end of the 1980s; a wave of bank runs comparable to those of the early 1930s (albeit mainly involving the shadow banking system rather than conventional banks); a liquidity trap in the United States, again reminiscent of Japan; and, most recently, a disruption of international capital flows and a wave of currency crises all too reminiscent of what happened to Asia in the late 1990s.

Let's tell the tale.

The Housing Bust and Its Fallout

The great U.S. housing boom began to deflate in the fall of 2005—but it took a while for most people to notice. As prices rose to the point where purchasing a home became out of reach for many Americans—even with no-down-payment, teaser-rate loans—sales began to slacken off. There was, as I wrote at the time, a hissing sound as air began to leak out of the bubble.

Yet housing prices kept rising for a while. This was to be expected. Houses aren't like stocks, with a single market price that changes minute by minute. Each house is unique, and sellers expect to wait a while before actually finding a buyer. As a result, prices tend to be based on what other houses have sold for in the recent past: sellers don't start cutting prices until it becomes painfully obvious that they aren't going to get a full-price offer. In 2005, after an extended period during which home prices had been rising sharply each year, sellers expected the trend to continue, so asking prices actually continued to rise for a while even as sales dropped.

By the late spring of 2006, however, the weakness of the market was starting to sink in. Prices began dropping, slowly at first, then with growing speed. By the second quarter of 2007, according to the widely used Case-Shiller home price index, prices were only down about 3 percent from their peak a year earlier. Over the course of the next year they fell more than 15 percent. The price declines were, of course, much larger in the regions that had experienced the biggest bubbles, like coastal Florida.

Even the gradual initial decline in home prices, however, undermined the assumptions on which the boom in subprime lending was based. Remember, the key rationale for this lending was the belief that it didn't really matter, from the lender's point of view, whether the borrower could actually make the mortgage payments: as long as home prices kept rising, troubled borrowers could always either refinance or pay off their mortgage by selling the house. As soon as home prices started falling instead of rising, and houses became hard to sell, default rates began rising. And at that point another ugly truth became apparent: foreclosure isn't just a tragedy for the homeowners, it's a lousy deal for the lender. Between the time it takes to get a foreclosed home back on the market, the legal expenses, the degradation that tends to happen in vacant homes, and so on, creditors seizing a house from the borrower typically get back only part, say half, of the original value of the loan.

In that case, you might ask, why not make a deal with the current homeowner to reduce payments and avoid the costs of foreclosure? Well, for one thing, that also costs money, and it requires staff. And subprime loans were not, for the most part, made by banks that held on to the loans; they were made by loan originators, who quickly sold the loans to financial institutions, which, in turn, sliced and diced pools of mortgages into collateralized debt obligations (CDOs) sold to investors. The actual management of the loans was left to loan servicers, who had neither the resources nor, for the most part, the incentive to engage in loan restructuring. And one more thing: the complexity of the financial engineering supporting subprime lending, which left ownership of mortgages dispersed among many investors with claims of varying seniority, created formidable legal obstacles to any kind of debt forgiveness.

So restructuring was mostly out, leading to costly foreclosures. And this meant that securities backed by subprime mortgages turned into very bad investments as soon as the housing boom began to falter.

The first moment of truth came early in 2007, as the trouble with subprime loans first became apparent. Recall that collateralized debt obligations established a seniority ranking for shares: owners of the more senior shares, the ones rating agencies declared to be AAA, had first dibs on payments, with those holding the less senior shares, which were given lower ratings, being paid only after the senior-share holders had received their due. Around February 2007 the realization sank in that the lower-rated shares were probably going to take serious losses, and prices of those shares plunged. This more or less put an end to the whole process of subprime lending: because nobody would buy the junior shares, it was no longer possible to repackage and sell subprime loans, and financing disappeared. This in turn, by removing an important source of housing demand, worsened the housing slump.

Still, for a long time investors believed that the senior shares in those CDOs were reasonably well protected. As late as October 2007, AAA-rated shares in subprime-backed mortgage pools were still trading at close to their face value. Eventually, however, it became clear that nothing related to housing was safe—not senior shares, not even loans made to borrowers with good credit ratings who made substantial down payments.

Why? Because of the sheer scale of the housing bubble. Nationally, housing was probably overvalued by more than 50 percent by the summer of 2006, which meant that to eliminate the overvaluation, prices would have to fall by a third. In some metropolitan areas, the overvaluation was much worse. In Miami, for example, home prices appeared to be at least twice as high as the fundamentals could justify. So in some areas prices could be expected to fall by 50 percent or more.

This meant that practically anyone who bought a house during the peak bubble years, even if he or she put 20 percent down, was going to end up with negative equity—with a mortgage worth more than the house. Indeed, there are probably around 12 million American homeowners with negative equity as this book goes to press. And homeowners with negative equity are prime candidates for default and foreclosure, no matter what their background. For one thing, some of them may simply choose to "walk away"—to walk out on their mortgage, figuring that they will end up ahead financially even after losing the house. It's never been clear how important a phenomenon walking away really is, but there are plenty of other routes to default. Job loss, unexpected medical expenses, divorce—all of these can leave a homeowner unable to make mortgage payments. And if the house is worth less than the mortgage, there is no way to make the lender whole.

As the severity of the housing bust sank in, it became clear that lenders would lose a lot of money, and so would the investors who bought mortgage-backed securities. But why should we cry for these people, as opposed to the homeowners themselves? After all, the end of the housing bubble will probably, when the final reckoning is made, have wiped out about $8 trillion of wealth. Of that, around $7 trillion will have been losses to homeowners, and only about $1 trillion losses to investors. Why obsess about that $1 trillion?

The answer is, because it has triggered the collapse of the shadow banking system.

The Non-Bank Banking Crisis

As we've seen, there were some serious financial tremors in the first half of 2007, but as late as early August the official view was that the problems posed by the housing slump and subprime loans were contained—and the strength of the stock market suggested that markets agreed with the official position. Then, not to put too fine a point on it, all hell broke loose. What happened?

In Chapter 8 I quoted Tim Geithner of the New York Federal Reserve Bank about the risks posed by the rise of the shadow banking system: "The scale of long-term risky and relatively illiquid assets financed by very short-term liabilities made many of the vehicles and institutions in this parallel financial system vulnerable to a classic type of run, but without the protections such as deposit insurance that the banking system has in place to reduce such risks." In that same speech, given in June 2008, he described—in surprisingly vivid language for a central banker—how that run had actually happened. It began with subprime-related losses, which undermined confidence in the shadow banking system. And this led to a vicious cycle of deleveraging:

> Once the investors in these financing arrangements—many conservatively managed money funds withdrew or threatened to withdraw their funds from these markets, the system became vulnerable to a self-reinforcing cycle of forced liquidation of assets, which further increased volatility and lowered prices across a variety of asset classes. In response, margin requirements were increased, or financing was withdrawn altogether from some customers, forcing more de-leveraging. Capital cushions eroded as assets were sold into distressed markets. The force of this dynamic was exacerbated by the

poor quality of assets—particularly mortgage-related assets—
that had been spread across the system. This helps explain
how a relatively small quantity of risky assets was able to
undermine the confidence of investors and other market participants across a much broader range of assets and markets.

Notice Geithner's emphasis on how declining asset values
damaged balance sheets, forcing further asset sales in a self-
reinforcing process. This is, at a fundamental level, the same logic
of deleveraging that led to the self-fulfilling financial crises in Asia
in 1997 and 1998, described in Chapter 4. Highly leveraged players in the economic system suffered losses, which forced them into
actions that led to further losses, and so on. In this case the losses
occurred through the collapsing value of risky financial assets rather
than through the collapsing value of the domestic currency, as in
Indonesia or Argentina, but the story was essentially the same.

And the result of this self-reinforcing process was, in effect, a
massive bank run that caused the shadow banking system to shrivel
up, much as the conventional banking system did in the early 1930s.
Auction-rate securities, in effect a banking sector providing $330 bil-
lion worth of credit, disappeared. Asset-backed commercial paper,
another de facto banking sector, dropped from providing $1.2 trillion
in credit to providing only $700 billion. And so on down the line.

Crazy things began happening in the financial markets. Interest
rates on U.S. Treasury bills—that is, short-term debt—dropped
close to zero. That was because investors were fleeing to safety,
and as one commentator put it, the only things they were willing
to buy were T-bills and bottled water. (U.S. government debt is as
safe as anything on the planet, not because the United States is
the most responsible nation on earth but because a world in which
the U.S. government collapses would be one in which pretty much

everything else collapses too—hence the demand for bottled water.) On a few occasions the interest rates on T-bills actually went negative, because they were the only thing people would accept as collateral in financial deals, and there was a scramble for the limited available supply.

Some borrowers were able to make up for the collapse of the shadow banking system by turning back to conventional banks for credit. One of the seemingly perverse aspects of the crisis has been an expansion of bank credit, which has confused some observers: where's the credit crunch, they ask? But the expansion of old-fashioned bank lending came nowhere near to making up for the collapse in shadow banking.

Consumer credit was the last to go, but by October 2008 there was growing evidence that credit cards were also on the chopping block, with credit limits cut, more applicants turned down, and the whole ability of American consumers, already feeling nervous, to charge things being undermined.

All across the economy, some businesses and individuals were losing access to credit, while others found themselves paying higher interest rates even as the Federal Reserve was trying to push rates down. And that brings us to the emergence of a Japan-style trap for U.S. monetary policy.

The Fed Loses Traction

By the time the financial crisis hit, Alan Greenspan was no longer running the Federal Reserve. In his place—and obliged to deal with the mess he left behind—was Ben Bernanke, a former economics professor at Princeton. (Bernanke was head of the Princeton economics department before leaving for the Fed, and hired me when I moved to Princeton from MIT.)

If you had to choose one individual to be in charge of the Fed during this crisis, that person would be Bernanke. He's a scholar of the Great Depression. His research on the way the banking crisis intensified the Depression led him to make a major theoretical contribution to monetary economics, focusing on the role of credit availability and balance sheet problems in restricting investment (mumble "Bernanke-Gertler" to a group of economists worriedly discussing the crisis, and they'll nod their heads knowingly). And he did extensive research on Japan's troubles in the 1990s. Nobody was more prepared, intellectually, for the mess we're in.

Yet as the crisis has unfolded, the Bernanke Fed has had a very hard time achieving any traction on either the financial markets or the economy as a whole.

The Fed is set up to do two main things: manage interest rates and, when necessary, provide cash to banks. It manages interest rates by buying Treasury bills from banks, thereby increasing their reserves, or selling T-bills to banks, thereby reducing their reserves. It provides cash to specific banks in times of need by lending them money directly. And it has used these tools aggressively since the crisis began. The Fed has cut the Federal funds rate—the overnight rate at which banks lend reserves to one another, which is the normal instrument of monetary policy—from 5.25 percent on the eve of the crisis to just 1 percent at the time of writing. "Total borrowings of depository institutions from the Federal Reserve," a measure of direct lending, have gone from near-zero before the crisis to more than $400 billion.

In normal times, these moves would have led to much easier credit. A fall in the Federal funds rate normally translates into reduced interest rates across the spectrum—lower interest rates on commercial credit, lower interest rates on corporate borrowing, lower mortgage rates. Meanwhile, lending to banks has historically been enough to ease any shortage of liquidity in the financial system. But these are not normal times, and historical precedents haven't applied.

The Fed's lack of traction is most apparent when it comes to riskier borrowers. Most obviously, there aren't any subprime loans being made now, shutting one whole class of potential home buyers out of the market. Businesses without a top credit rating are paying higher interest rates for short-term credit now than they did before the crisis, even though the interest rates the Fed controls have fallen by more than four percentage points. The interest rate on Baa-rated corporate bonds at the time of writing was above 9 percent, compared with about 6.5 percent before the crisis. Down the line, the interest rates that matter for spending and investment decisions have risen or at least failed to fall, in spite of the Fed's attempt to drive rates down.

Even prime mortgage borrowers have been hit: the thirty-year mortgage rate is still roughly where it was in the summer of 2007. That's because the crisis in the financial system more or less knocked private lenders out of the market, leaving only Fannie Mae and Freddie Mac, the government-sponsored lenders, still in business. And Fannie and Freddie found themselves in trouble too: they hadn't made as many bad loans as the private sector, but they had made some, and they had very thin capital bases. In September 2008 the federal government took control of Fannie and Freddie, which should have eased concerns about their debt and reduced mortgage rates. But the Bush administration made a point of denying that Fannie/Freddie debt was backed by the full faith of the U.S. government, so that even after nationalization they continued to have trouble raising funds.

What about all the loans the Federal Reserve made to the banks? They have probably helped, but not as much as one might have expected, because conventional banks aren't at the heart of the crisis. Here's an example: if auction-rate security arrangements had been part of the conventional banking system, the issuers would have been able to borrow from the Fed when too few private investors showed up at the auctions; as a result, the auctions wouldn't have failed and the sector wouldn't have collapsed. Because they weren't part of conventional banks, however, the auctions did fail and the sector did collapse, and no amount of Fed loans to Citibank or Bank of America could do anything to halt the process.

In effect, then, the Fed found itself presiding over a Japan-style liquidity trap, in which conventional monetary policy had lost all traction over the real economy. True, the Fed funds rate hadn't been cut all the way to zero, but there was little reason to think that cutting one more percentage point would have much impact.

What else could the Fed do? In 2004, in scholarly work, Bernanke had argued that monetary policy could be effective, even in a liquidity trap, if one were willing to "alter the composition of the central bank's balance sheet." Instead of only holding Treasury bills and loans to conventional banks, the Fed could make loans to other players: investment banks, money-market funds, maybe even nonfinancial businesses. And over the course of 2008 the Fed introduced an alphabet soup of special lending "facilities" to do just that: the TSLF, the PDCF, and so on. In October 2008 the Fed announced that it would begin buying commercial paper too, in effect proposing to do the lending the private financial system wouldn't or couldn't do.

It remains possible, at the time of writing, that these schemes will eventually bear fruit. What one has to say, however, is that their effects so far have been disappointing. Why? I'd argue that the problem is one of substitution and scale. When the Fed acts to increase the quantity of bank reserves, it's doing something no other institution can do: only the Fed can create monetary base, which can be used as cash in circulation or held as bank reserves. Furthermore, its actions tend to be large relative to the scale of the asset classes involved, since the monetary base is "only" $800 billion. When the Fed tries to support the credit market more broadly, by contrast, it's doing something private actors also do— which means that the credit it pumps into the system may be partly offset by private withdrawals—and it's also trying to move a much bigger beast, the $50 trillion or so credit market.

The Bernanke Fed has also suffered from the problem of being, again and again, behind the curve. The financial crisis keeps developing new dimensions, which few people—including the very smart people at the Fed—see coming. And that brings me to the international dimension of the crisis.

The Mother of All Currency Crises

After the financial crises of 1997 and 1998, the governments of the affected countries tried to protect themselves against a repeat performance. They avoided the foreign borrowing that had made them vulnerable to a cutoff of overseas funding. They built up huge war chests of dollars and euros, which were supposed to protect them in the event of any future emergency. And the conventional wisdom was that the "emerging markets"—Brazil, Russia, India, China, and a host of smaller economies, including the victims of the 1997 crisis—were now "decoupled" from the United States, able to keep growing despite the mess in America. "Decoupling is no myth," *The Economist* assured its readers back in March. "Indeed, it may yet save the world economy."

Unfortunately, that doesn't seem likely. On the contrary, says Stephen Jen, the chief currency strategist at Morgan Stanley, the "hard landing" in emerging markets may become the "second epi-center" of the global crisis (U.S. financial markets were the first).

What happened? Alongside the growth of the shadow banking system, there was another transformation in the character of the financial system over the past fifteen years, with much of it taking place after the Asian crisis—namely, the rise of financial globaliza-tion, with investors in each country holding large stakes in other countries. In 1996, on the eve of the Asian crisis, the United States had assets overseas equal to 52 percent of GDP, and liabilities equal to 57 percent of GDP. By 2007, these numbers were up to 128 percent and 145 percent, respectively. The United States had moved deeper into net debtor status; but the net is less impressive than the vast increase in cross-holdings.

Like much of what happened to the financial system over the past decade or two, this change was supposed to reduce risk: because U.S. investors held much of their wealth abroad, they were less exposed to a slump in America, and because foreign investors held much of their wealth in the United States, they were less exposed to a slump overseas. But a large part of the increase in financial globalization actually came from the investments of highly lever-aged financial institutions, which were making various sorts of risky cross-border bets. And when things went wrong in the United States, these cross-border investments acted as what economists call a "transmission mechanism," allowing a crisis that started with the U.S. housing market to drive fresh rounds of crises overseas. The failure of hedge funds associated with a French bank is gener-ally considered to have marked the beginning of the crisis; by the fall of 2008, the troubles of housing loans in places like Florida had destroyed the banking system of Iceland.

In the case of the emerging markets, there was a special point of vulnerability, the so-called carry trade. This trade involves borrowing in countries with low interest rates, especially but not only Japan, and lending in places with high interest rates, like Brazil and Russia. It was a highly profitable trade as long as nothing went wrong; but eventually something did.

The triggering event seems to have been the fall of Lehman Brothers, the investment bank, on September 15, 2008. When Bear Stearns, another of the original five major investment banks, got in trouble in March 2008, the Fed and the Treasury moved in— not to rescue the firm, which disappeared, but to protect the firm's "counterparties," those to whom it owed money or with whom it had made financial deals. There was a widespread expectation that Lehman would receive the same treatment. But the Treasury Department decided that the consequences of a Lehman failure would not be too severe, and allowed the firm to go under without any protection for its counterparties.

Within days it was clear that this had been a disastrous move: confidence plunged further, asset prices fell off another cliff, and the few remaining working channels of credit dried up. The effective nationalization of AIG, the giant insurer, a few days later, failed to stem the panic.

And one of the casualties of the latest round of panic was the carry trade. The conduit of funds from Japan and other low-interest nations was cut off, leading to a round of self-reinforcing effects all too familiar from the crisis of 1997. Because capital was no longer flowing out of Japan, the value of the yen soared; because capital was no longer flowing into emerging markets, the value of emerging-market currencies plunged. This led to large capital losses for whoever had borrowed in one currency and lent in another. In some cases that meant hedge funds—and the hedge fund industry, which had held up better than expected until the demise of Lehman Brothers, began shrinking rapidly. In other cases it meant firms in emerging markets, which had borrowed cheaply abroad, suddenly faced big losses.

For it turned out that the efforts of emerging-market governments to protect themselves against another crisis had been undone by the private sector's obliviousness to risk. In Russia, for example, banks and corporations rushed to borrow abroad because foreign interest rates were lower than ruble rates. So while the Russian government was accumulating an impressive $560 billion hoard of foreign exchange, Russian corporations and banks were running up an almost equally impressive $460 billion foreign debt. Then, suddenly, these corporations and banks found their credit lines cut off, and the ruble value of their debts surging. And nobody was safe: for example, major Brazilian banks avoided taking on a large foreign exposure but nonetheless found themselves in trouble because their domestic clients hadn't been equally careful.

It all bore a strong resemblance to previous currency crises— Indonesia 1997, Argentina 2002. But it was on a far larger scale. This, truly, is the mother of all currency crises, and it represents a fresh disaster for the world's financial system.

A Global Slump

Most of this chapter has been taken up with the financial aspects of the crisis. What does all this portend for the "real economy," the economy of jobs, wages, and production? Nothing good.

The United States, Britain, Spain, and several other countries probably would have suffered recessions when their housing bubbles burst even if the financial system hadn't broken down. Falling home prices have a direct negative effect on employment through the decline in construction, and they tend to lead to reduced consumer spending because consumers feel poorer and lose access to home equity loans; these negatives have a multiplier effect as falling employment leads to further declines in spending. That said, the U.S. economy actually held up fairly well at first in the face of the housing bust, mainly because the weakness of the dollar led to rising exports, which helped offset the decline in construction.

But the financial collapse seems certain to turn what might have been a run-of-the-mill recession—the U.S. employment rate began to drop at the end of 2007, but until September 2008 the decline was fairly modest—into something much, much worse. The intensification of the credit crisis after the fall of Lehman Brothers, the sudden crisis in emerging markets, a collapse in consumer confidence as the scale of the financial mess hit the headlines, all point to the worst recession in the United States, and in the world as a whole, since the early 1980s. And many economists will be relieved if it's only that bad.

And what's really worrying is the loss of policy traction. The recession of 1981–82, which drove the unemployment rate above 10 percent, was a terrible thing, but it was also more or less a deliberate choice: the Fed pursued a tight-money policy to break the back of inflation, and as soon as Fed Chairman Paul Volcker decided the economy had suffered enough, he undid the screws, and the economy came roaring back. Economic devastation turned into "morning in America" with startling speed.

This time, by contrast, the economy is stalling despite repeated efforts by policymakers to get it going again. This policy helplessness is reminiscent of Japan in the 1990s. It's also reminiscent of the 1930s. We're not in a depression now, and despite everything, I don't think we're heading into one (although I'm not as sure of that as I'd like to be). We are, however, well into the realm of depression economics.

10

THE RETURN OF
DEPRESSION ECONOMICS

The world economy is not in depression; it probably won't fall into depression, despite the magnitude of the current crisis (although I wish I was completely sure about that). But while depression itself has not returned, depression economics—the kinds of problems that characterized much of the world economy in the 1930s but have not been seen since—has staged a stunning comeback. Fifteen years ago hardly anybody thought that modern nations would be forced to endure bone-crushing recessions for fear of currency speculators, and that major advanced nations would find themselves persistently unable to generate enough spending to keep their workers and factories employed. The world economy has turned out to be a much more dangerous place than we imagined.

How did the world become this dangerous? More important, how do we get out of the current crisis, and what can we do to prevent such crises from happening in the first place? In this book I have told many stories; now it is time to try to draw some morals.

What Is Depression Economics?

What does it mean to say that depression economics has returned? Essentially it means that for the first time in two generations, failures on the demand side of the economy—insufficient private spending to make use of the available productive capacity—have become the clear and present limitation on prosperity for a large part of the world.

We—by which I mean not only economists but also policymakers and the educated public at large—weren't ready for this. The specific set of foolish ideas that has laid claim to the name "supply-side economics" is a crank doctrine that would have had little influence if it did not appeal to the prejudices of editors and wealthy men. But over the past few decades there has been a steady drift in emphasis in economic thinking away from the demand side to the supply side of the economy.

This drift was partly the result of theoretical disputes within economics that—as they so often do—gradually filtered out, in somewhat garbled form, into wider discourse. Briefly, the source of the theoretical disputes was this: in principle, shortfalls of overall demand would cure themselves if only wages and prices fell rapidly in the face of unemployment. In the story of the depressed baby-sitting co-op, one way the situation could have resolved itself would have been for the price of an hour of baby-sitting in terms of coupons to fall, so that the purchasing power of the existing supply of coupons would have risen, and the co-op would have returned to "full employment" without any action by its management. In reality prices don't fall quickly in the face of recession, but economists have been unable to agree about exactly why. The result has been a series of bitter academic battles that have made the whole subject of recessions and how they happen a sort of professional minefield in which ever fewer economists dare to tread. And the public has understandably concluded either that economists don't understand recessions or that demand-side remedies have been discredited. The truth is that good old-fashioned demand-side macroeconomics has a lot to offer in our current predicament—but its defenders lack all conviction, while its critics are filled with a passionate intensity.

Paradoxically, if the theoretical weaknesses of demand-side economics are one reason we were unready for the return of depression-type issues, its practical successes are another. During all the decades that economists have argued with one another over whether monetary policy can actually be used to get an economy out of a recession, central banks have repeatedly gone ahead and used it to do just that—so effectively in fact that the idea of a prolonged economic slump due to insufficient demand became implausible. Surely the Federal Reserve and its counterparts in other countries could always cut interest rates enough to keep spending high; except in the very short run, then, the only limitation on economic performance was an economy's ability to produce—that is, the supply side.

Even now, many economists still think of recessions as a minor issue, their study as a faintly disreputable subject. Robert Lucas's presidential address, which I quoted in Chapter 1, explicitly made the case that the business cycle was no longer an important subject, and that economists should shift their attention to technological progress and long-run growth. These are fine, important issues, and in the long run they are what really matter—but as Keynes pointed out, in the long run we are all dead.

Meanwhile, in the short run the world is lurching from crisis to crisis, all of them crucially involving the problem of generating sufficient demand. Japan from the early 1990s onward, Mexico in 1995, Mexico, Thailand, Malaysia, Indonesia, and Korea in 1997, Argentina in 2002, and just about everyone in 2008—one country after another has experienced a recession that at least temporarily undoes years of economic progress, and finds that the conventional policy responses don't seem to have any effect. Once again, the question of how to create enough demand to make use of the economy's capacity has become crucial. Depression economics is back.

What to Do: Dealing with the Emergency

What the world needs right now is a rescue operation. The global credit system is in a state of paralysis, and a global slump is building momentum as I write this. Reform of the weaknesses that made this crisis possible is essential, but it can wait a little while. First, we need to deal with the clear and present danger. To do this, policymakers around the world need to do two things: get credit flowing again and prop up spending.

The first task is the harder of the two, but it must be done, and soon. Hardly a day goes by without news of some further disaster wreaked by the freezing up of credit. As I wrote this draft, for example, reports were coming in of the collapse of letters of credit, the key financing method for world trade. Suddenly, buyers of imports, especially in developing countries, can't carry through on their deals, and ships are standing idle: the Baltic Dry Index, a widely used measure of shipping costs, has fallen 89 percent this year.

What lies behind the credit squeeze is the combination of reduced trust in and decimated capital at financial institutions. People and institutions, including the financial institutions, don't want to deal with anyone unless they have substantial capital to back up their promises, yet the crisis has depleted capital across the board.

The obvious solution is to put in more capital. In fact, that's a standard response in financial crises. In 1933 the Roosevelt administration used the Reconstruction Finance Corporation to recapitalize banks by buying preferred stock—stock that had seniority over common stock in terms of its claims on profits. When Sweden experienced a financial crisis in the early 1990s, the government stepped in and provided the banks with additional capital equal to 4 percent of the country's GDP—the equivalent of about $600 billion for the United States today—in return for a partial ownership. When Japan moved to rescue its banks in 1998, it purchased more than $500 billion in preferred stock, the equivalent relative to GDP of around a $2 trillion capital injection in the United States. In each case, the provision of capital helped restore the ability of banks to lend, and unfroze the credit markets.

A financial rescue along similar lines is now underway in the United States and other advanced economies, although it was late in coming, thanks in part to the ideological tilt of the Bush administration. At first, after the fall of Lehman Brothers, the Treasury Department proposed buying up $700 billion in troubled assets from banks and other financial institutions. Yet it was never clear how this was supposed to help the situation. (If the Treasury paid market value, it would do little to help the banks' capital position, while if it paid above-market value it would stand accused of throwing taxpayers' money away.) Never mind: after dithering for three weeks, the United States followed the lead already set first by Britain and then by continental European countries, and turned the plan into a recapitalization scheme.

It seems doubtful, however, that this will be enough to turn things around, for at least three reasons. First, even if the full $700 billion is used for recapitalization (so far only a fraction has been committed), it will still be small, relative to GDP, compared with the Japanese bank bailout—and it's arguable that the severity of the financial crisis in the United States and Europe now rivals that of Japan. Second, it's still not clear how much of the bailout will reach the shadow banking system, the core of the problem. Third, it's not clear whether banks will be willing to lend out the funds, as opposed to sitting on them (a problem encountered by the New Deal seventy-five years ago).

My guess is that the recapitalization will eventually have to get bigger and broader, and that there will eventually have to be more assertion of government control—in effect, it will come closer to a full temporary nationalization of a significant part of the financial system. Just to be clear, this isn't a long-term goal, a matter of seizing the economy's commanding heights: finance should be reprivatized as soon as it's safe to do so, just as Sweden put banking back in the private sector after its big bailout in the early nineties. But for now the important thing is to loosen up credit by any means at hand, without getting tied up in ideological knots. Nothing could be worse than failing to do what's necessary out of fear that acting to save the financial system is somehow "socialist."

The same goes for another line of approach to resolving the credit crunch: getting the feds, temporarily, into the business of lending directly to the nonfinancial sector. The Federal Reserve's willingness to buy commercial paper is a major step in this direction, but more will probably be necessary.

All these actions should be coordinated with other advanced countries. The reason is the globalization of finance, described in Chapter 9. Part of the payoff to U.S. rescues of the financial system is that they help loosen up access to credit in Europe; part of the payoff to European rescue efforts is that they loosen up credit here. So everyone should be doing more or less the same thing; we're all in this together.

And one more thing: the spread of the financial crisis to emerging markets makes a global rescue for developing countries part of the solution to the crisis. As with recapitalization, parts of this were already in place at the time of writing: the International Monetary Fund was providing loans to countries with troubled economies like Ukraine, with less of the moralizing and demands for austerity that it engaged in during the Asian crisis of the 1990s. Meanwhile, the Fed provided swap lines to several emerging-market central banks, giving them the right to borrow dollars as needed. As with recapitalization, the efforts so far look as if they're in the right direction but too small, so more will be needed.

Even if the rescue of the financial system starts to bring credit markets back to life, we'll still face a global slump that's gathering momentum. What should be done about that? The answer, almost surely, is good old Keynesian fiscal stimulus.

Now, the United States tried a fiscal stimulus in early 2008; both the Bush administration and congressional Democrats touted it as a plan to "jump-start" the economy. The actual results were, however, disappointing, for two reasons. First, the stimulus was too small, accounting for only about 1 percent of GDP. The next one should be much bigger, say, as much as 4 percent of GDP. Second, most of the money in the first package took the form of tax rebates, many of which were saved rather than spent. The next plan should focus on sustaining and expanding government spending—sustaining it by providing aid to state and local governments, expanding it with spending on roads, bridges, and other forms of infrastructure.

The usual objection to public spending as a form of economic stimulus is that it takes too long to get going—that by the time the boost to demand arrives, the slump is over. That doesn't seem to be a major worry now, however: it's very hard to see any quick economic recovery, unless some unexpected new bubble arises to replace the housing bubble. (A headline in the satirical newspaper *The Onion* captured the problem perfectly: "Recession-Plagued Nation Demands New Bubble to Invest In.") As long as public spending is pushed along with reasonable speed, it should arrive in plenty of time to help—and it has two great advantages over tax breaks. On one side, the money would actually be spent; on the other, something of value (e.g., bridges that don't fall down) would be created.

Some readers may object that providing a fiscal stimulus through public works spending is what Japan did in the 1990s—and it is. Even in Japan, however, public spending probably prevented a weak economy from plunging into an actual depression. There are, moreover, reasons to believe that stimulus through public spending would work better in the United States, if done promptly, than it did in Japan. For one thing, we aren't yet stuck in the trap of deflationary expectations that Japan fell into after years of insufficiently forceful policies. And Japan waited far too long to recapitalize its banking system, a mistake we hopefully won't repeat.

The point in all of this is to approach the current crisis in the spirit that we'll do whatever it takes to turn things around; if what has been done so far isn't enough, do more and do something different, until credit starts to flow and the real economy starts to recover.

And once the recovery effort is well underway, it will be time to turn to prophylactic measures: reforming the system so that the crisis doesn't happen again.

Financial Reform

We have magneto trouble, said John Maynard Keynes at the start of the Great Depression: most of the economic engine was in good shape, but a crucial component, the financial system, wasn't working. He also said this: "We have involved ourselves in a colossal muddle, having blundered in the control of a delicate machine, the working of which we do not understand." Both statements are as true now as they were then.

How did this second great colossal muddle arise? In the aftermath of the Great Depression, we redesigned the machine so that we *did* understand it, well enough at any rate to avoid big disasters. Banks, the piece of the system that malfunctioned so badly in the 1930s, were placed under tight regulation and supported by a strong safety net. Meanwhile, international movements of capital, which played a disruptive role in the 1930s, were also limited. The financial system became a little boring but much safer.

Then things got interesting and dangerous again. Growing international capital flows set the stage for devastating currency crises in the 1990s and for a globalized financial crisis in 2008. The growth of the shadow banking system, without any corresponding extension of regulation, set the stage for latter-day bank runs on a massive scale. These runs involved frantic mouse clicks rather than frantic mobs outside locked bank doors, but they were no less devastating.

What we're going to have to do, clearly, is relearn the lessons our grandfathers were taught by the Great Depression. I won't try to lay out the details of a new regulatory regime, but the basic principle should be clear: anything that has to be rescued during a financial crisis, because it plays an essential role in the financial mechanism, should be regulated when there *isn't* a crisis so that it doesn't take excessive risks. Since the 1930s commercial banks have been required to have adequate capital, hold reserves of liquid assets that can be quickly converted into cash, and limit the types of investments they make, all in return for federal guarantees when things go wrong. Now that we've seen a wide range of non-bank institutions create what amounts to a banking crisis, comparable regulation has to be extended to a much larger part of the system.

We're also going to have to think hard about how to deal with financial globalization. In the aftermath of the Asian crisis of the 1990s, there were some calls for long-term restrictions on international capital flows, not just temporary controls in times of crisis. For the most part these calls were rejected in favor of a strategy of building up large foreign exchange reserves that were supposed to stave off future crises. Now it seems that this strategy didn't work. For countries like Brazil and Korea, it must seem like a nightmare: after all that they've done, they're going through the 1990s crisis all over again. Exactly what form the next response should take isn't clear, but financial globalization has definitely turned out to be even more dangerous than we realized.

The Power of Ideas

As readers may have gathered, I believe not only that we're living in a new era of depression economics, but also that John Maynard Keynes—the economist who made sense of the Great Depression—is now more relevant than ever. Keynes concluded his masterwork, *The General Theory of Employment, Interest and Money*, with a famous disquisition on the importance of economic ideas: "Soon or late, it is ideas, not vested interests, which are dangerous for good or evil."

We can argue about whether that's always true, but in times like these, it definitely is. The quintessential economic sentence is supposed to be "There is no free lunch"; it says that there are limited resources, that to have more of one thing you must accept less of another, that there is no gain without pain. Depression economics, however, is the study of situations where there *is* a free lunch, if we can only figure out how to get our hands on it, because there are unemployed resources that could be put to work. The true scarcity in Keynes's world—and ours—was therefore not of resources, or even of virtue, but of understanding.

We will not achieve the understanding we need, however, unless we are willing to think clearly about our problems and to follow those thoughts wherever they lead. Some people say that our economic problems are structural, with no quick cure available; but I believe that the only important structural obstacles to world prosperity are the obsolete doctrines that clutter the minds of men.

EPILOGUE: THE GREAT RECESSION

In the hardcover edition of this book I warned that the world economy was experiencing conditions "reminiscent of the 1930s." By the time this epilogue was written (June 2009) the resemblance had become all too close. Over the past year, by a number of measures, the world has experienced a slump every bit as severe as the first year of the Great Depression.

The figure below, taken from work by the economic historians Barry Eichengreen and Kevin O'Rourke, shows one such measure: world industrial production. One year into the current slump, which Eichengreen and O'Rourke say began in April 2008, the world was closely tracking the plunge that took place in the first year of the Great Depression.

Needless to say, this slump has led to mass unemployment. In the United States the official unemployment rate hit 9.4 percent in May 2009—not quite a post-Depression record (yet), but a number of indicators, like a surge in involuntary part-time work, suggest that the jobs picture is even worse than it looks. Other countries have been even harder hit. In Spain, for example, the unemployment rate is 18 percent and rising.

WORLD INDUSTRIAL PRODUCTION

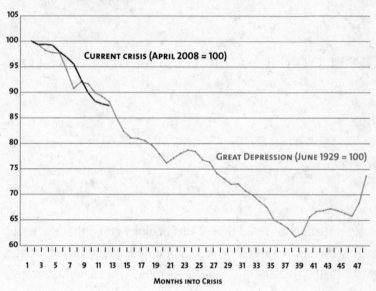

* Source: "A Tale of Two Depressions" at www.VoxEU.org by Barry Eichengreen, University of California, Berkeley, and Kevin O'Rourke, Trinity College Dublin. Reproduced with permission.

Many observers are already calling this the Great Recession. But as the figure shows, what made the Great Depression so great was the fact that the slump just kept going—the awful first year was followed by equally awful second and third years. Will that happen again? Will the Great Recession turn into another Great Depression?

Probably not. One big difference between 2009 and 1930 is that this time policymakers know just how bad things could get, and the prospect of a second Great Depression has concentrated their minds. The Federal Reserve and, to a lesser extent, its counterparts in other nations have moved aggressively to expand credit, with the result that its assets have ballooned from $800 billion to more than $2 trillion.

Governments have also been much more willing to run budget deficits than they were in the 1930s. Only the United States and China (how's that for an odd couple?) are pursuing large WPA-style spending to bolster their economies, but most nations have at least avoided doing the Herbert Hoover thing of raising taxes and cutting spending as the economy slumps.

And at the time of writing things seem to be looking a bit better. Or to be more accurate, the rate at which things are getting worse seems to be slowing. For example, the United States is still losing hundreds of thousands of jobs each month—but it isn't losing jobs as fast as it was earlier this year. The sense that the world economy was plunging uncontrollably into the abyss has eased.

While the risk of total economic collapse seems to be receding, that's a long way from saying that the crisis is over. Think of the world economy as a patient who was rushed to the hospital and seemed to be at risk of dying. Now the patient is off the critical list but is still very, very ill—with no hint of when a full recovery might happen. The odds that the world will face a Japanese-style period of extended weakness, maybe even a lost decade, still seem high.

One thing making those odds even higher is the growing backlash against government intervention.

Students of the Great Depression often use the events of 1937 as a cautionary tale. By then the U.S. economy had been growing rapidly for four years, although unemployment was still very high by normal standards. Nonetheless, American policymakers declared victory over the depression and tried to return to normal, orthodox economic policies. FDR tried to balance the budget; the Federal Reserve tried to "mop up" what it considered the excess reserves of banks. The result was disaster: the economy slumped again, unemployment soared, and people began talking about the "Roosevelt depression." Full recovery had to wait until World War II.

Sure enough, the first signs of economic "green shoots" have led to demands for a return to orthodoxy. Pundits, ignoring the lessons of both Japan in the 1990s and America in the 1930s, incessantly warn that the expansion of Federal Reserve credit will cause inflation and that budget deficits will crowd out business investment. If policymakers give in to such complaints, it will be 1937 all over again.

So it's crucial to appreciate where we are. We may have avoided a repeat of the Great Depression, but we're still very much living in a world in which the usual rules of economic policy don't apply. That is, we're living in a world governed by depression economics— and our understanding of the logic of depression economics, in which virtue can be vice and prudence folly, is our only defense against economic disaster.

Index

ABOUT THE AUTHOR

Paul Krugman is the recipient of the 2008 Nobel Prize in Economics. The author of a twice-weekly column for the op-ed page of the *New York Times* and a daily blog, "The Conscience of a Liberal," derived from his book of the same name, Krugman has been named Columnist of the Year by *Editor and Publisher* magazine. He is a professor of economics and international affairs at Princeton University, and is the author or editor of twenty books and more than two hundred professional journal articles. For more information, please visit Krugmanonline.com.